MW00955851

Athens Guide: The Most Interesting Places in the Greek Capital for Three Days!

The Freshest and Most Up-to-Date Information for the Year 2024.

By George Esperidis

Table of Contents

Introduction

Suppose you are holding this book in your hands. In that case, chances are you're a seasoned traveler, meticulously planning your trip and seeking vivid experiences and new and intriguing knowledge. In that case, my friend, this guide is just what you need! My name is George Esperidis, and I am a native Athenian, an art historian, a medievalist, and a Byzantinist. With my guide, "Athens Guide: The Most Interesting Places in the Greek Capital for Three Days!" we will embark on a fascinating trip through my hometown – one of the oldest in Europe – and witness its inception in antiquity, its flourishing in ancient times, decline in the early era, and its rebirth from the ashes in the 19th century. But besides the captivating stories about Athens and its inhabitants, in my guide, you will find:

1. The city's best cafes, restaurants, taverns, and bars (only the most up-to-date information for 2024). Helpful tips on choosing neighborhoods to stay in, ensuring nothing hinders your enjoyment of Athens!

2. Advice on purchasing transportation tickets and many other details often overlooked in other guides but crucial for any traveler!

My guide presents a walking itinerary through Athens that is designed for three days. It is important to note that I do not include time for visiting museums in my itinerary, as this is a very personal matter. For example, some may be interested only in the archaeological museum, where one could spend an entire day. In contrast, others may want to enjoy several museums but only view the main exhibits. Thus, I have allowed my readers to plan their museum excursions themselves. I also consider it my duty to mention that all the information in the guide is reliable and for entertainment purposes. Thank you for choosing this handbook, and I wish you a pleasant holiday in Athens!

Yours sincerely,
George Esperidis

1. Acropolis of Athens
2. Areopagus
3. Ancient Athens Agora
4. Athens Observatory
5. Monastiraki Square and Hadrian's Library
6. Roman Agora
7. Metropolis Square
8. Ermu Street
9. Syndagmatos Square (Syndagma)
10. Anaphiotika
11. Old Royal Palace (Parliament)
12. National Garden (Royal Garden)
13. New Royal Palace

14. Prime Minister's Residence
15. Kolonaki Square
16. Cathedral of St. Dionysius (Orthodox)
17. Lycabettos Hill
18. Archaeological Museum
19. Omonia Square
20. Central Market (Varvakeios)
21. National Historical Museum
22. Square of Tears
23. Neoclassical Trilogy
24. Zappeion Exhibition Hall
25. Temple of Olympian Zeus
26. Kallimarmaro Olympic Stadium

A Brief History of Athens – a City of Myths.

If we were to believe ancient myths (which we won't), Athens was founded by King Cecrops I, a being born of the Earth herself (the Goddess Gaia), possessing a human torso and serpent tail instead of legs. Cecrops was revered as the founder not only of Athens but also of the entire Attica region. According to the myth, he ruled in those ancient times when people did not yet know how to make wine, so ritual libations in honor of the Gods were performed with water. That's why he

King Cecrops I

was placed in the sky as the Aquarius constellation. His myths also attribute him to being the builder of the Athenian Acropolis, where a contest between the Goddess Athena and the God Poseidon took place to decide the city's patron deity. Cecrops proposed that each city should offer something useful for its future inhabitants. Poseidon struck the rock with his trident, causing a spring of salty water to gush forth, which was neither suitable for drinking nor irrigation.Conversely, Athena planted an olive tree seed in the rock next to the spring, which grew and provided shade, wood, and tasty fruits. Victory was awarded to Athena, and the city was named Athens in her honor. According to the tale,

Poseidon, resentful of this decision, punished Athens with droughts yearly after that. Of course, this is nothing more than a beautiful legend. Still, archaeological findings on the Acropolis indicate that the history of the first settlements in the area of the modern-day Greek capital dates back to the 4th millennium BCE, or 5000 years ago. By the 15th century BCE (3400 years ago), there existed a large fortress on the Acropolis, belonging to the ancient and quite developed Mycenaean civilization, which is closely associated with the famous myth of the Trojan War (it was here that Mycenaeans clashed with Trojans). The Mycenaean civilization was destroyed in the 13th century BCE due to the invasion of the Dorians, barbarian tribes that destroyed most of the major Mycenaean cities and initiated the so-called "Bronze Age Collapse," a period lasting about 500 years, during which civilization in the territory of modern Greece was reset to "zero," as the Dorians did not know writing, metalworking, weaving, pottery, or even how to work with clay. However, ancient Athenians insisted that, unlike the inhabitants of the Peloponnese (mostly Spartans), they did not undergo "Dorization" and remained pure-blooded Ionians, although archaeological evidence suggests that throughout the 13th and early 12th centuries BCE, the city was in a state of decline. Nevertheless, by the 10th century BCE, Athens became a significant trading center again. The presence of the impregnable fortress – the Athenian Acropolis – and access to the sea gave Athens an advantage that its leading rivals – Sparta and Thebes – did not have. At that time, Athens was ruled by ancient kings, of whom many aristocratic families later claimed descent. For example, the ancestor of the philosopher Plato and the famous reformer Solon was the last King of Athens, Codrus, who ruled from 1089 to 1068 BCE. The residence of the Athenian Kings was the Acropolis, and I recommend you remember this fact. Then, in the 9th to 8th centuries BCE, Athens transitioned from a monarchical to an aristocratic form of government, in which all power was concentrated in the hands of the aristocrats – representatives of the city's most noble and influential families. Initially, they organized something akin to a parliament under the Athenian King, limiting his power (this parliament met on the preserved hill of Areopagus near the Acropolis). Afterwards, the aristocrats elected a lifelong archon to replace the King. This system gradually led Athens to a deep social crisis, where all wealth and power ended up in the hands of a minority, forming a closed upper class that did not admit new members. The era of Athenian democracy began after the reforms of Solon in the early 6th century BCE, as a result of which the barbaric practice of debt slavery was abolished. All citizens of the city-state were divided into four classes based on their income, and the poorest class, which made up the majority of Athens' population, gained political rights and the ability to vote on important issues at the popular assembly, the "Ecclesia," which convened on the Pnyx hill near the Areopagus. The latter's powers were reduced, and the highest governing body became the Council of Four Hundred, comprising representatives from all classes except the poorest. Thus, the first democratic system in the history of mankind emerged, which, although oligarchic, was still much better than the aristocracy that had existed before. However, this democracy did not last long. In the mid-6th century BCE, during the rule of the tyrant Pisistratus (also a relative of the Ancient Kings of Athens who seized power in Athens through a military coup in 560 BCE), the first major temple dedicated to Athena appeared on the Acropolis, the Hecatompedon, or "Temple in a Hundred Steps," built on the foundation of the ancient Mycenaean Royal Palace from the 14th century BCE. Also, during Pisistratus' reign, Athens saw the establishment of the first clay water pipeline, bringing water from underground sources in the mountains of Hymettus, which surrounded Athens from the east and northeast, as well as from the Ilissos River, which today is completely channeled underground and surfaces only as a small stream in the park near the Temple of Olympian Zeus's remains. After Pisistratus' death, his power was divided between his sons – Hipparchus and Hippias, who were soon overthrown by two popular uprisings. As a result, under the leadership of the aristocrat Cleisthenes, Athens became a true democracy in 508 BCE. In 480 and 479 BCE, during the Greco-Persian Wars, the city was plundered and burned twice by the Persians. Among the destroyed temples was the Temple of the Goddess Athena Hecatompedon. Subsequently, construction works for the current Parthenon took place on the Acropolis for about thirty years. This period marked the beginning of the so-called "Golden Age of Pericles," during which Athens became the leading power of the Hellenistic world, dominating the seas and leading the largest military alliance in Ancient Greece. This era ended with Athens' defeat in the Peloponnesian War against Sparta in 404 BCE. In 338 BCE, after Athens' crushing defeat at the Battle of Chaeronea against the forces of the King of Macedonia, Philip II (the father of Alexander the Great), the city retreated definitively in terms of military and political significance. However, it retained its wealth and status as the cultural center of Ancient Greece. In 88-85 BCE, much of Athens was destroyed by the Roman general Sulla, who

View of Athens from Lycabettus Hill, 2024.

captured the city and initiated the Roman era of Athenian history. Unlike other conquered ancient Greek cities, Athens was granted the status of a free city because Athenian schools (Plato's Academy, Socrates' Academy, and others) were highly respected, and even Romans studied in them. Despite the bloody conquest of the city, for the next 500 years, Athens remained an important cultural and scientific center, especially favored by Emperors Hadrian and Nero. In the years 267 and 396 CE, Athens was plundered and burned by Germanic-speaking barbarians – the Heruli and the Visigoths. These two events left a significant mark on the city's history: remnants of fortifications hastily built by the Athenians in the 3rd century CE in anticipation of the Germanic invasions can be found in various parts of the old city. Despite the colossal destruction and population decline after these two raids, up to the reign of Emperor

Seal of Duke Otto de la Roche
During the rule of the House of La Roche, maritime piracy was a significant source of income for the Duchy of Athens. The port city of Nafplion in Argolis, owned by the La Roches, served as the largest base for corsairs of that time. However, even the Byzantine Emperors were not averse to hiring pirates to hinder Franco-Venetian trade in the Mediterranean.

Justinian I (527-565 CE), Athens retained its status as the "mother of Greek culture," where Neoplatonism — a renaissance of Plato's philosophical teachings — mainly flourished. In the early 5th century CE, Christianity arrived in Athens. In 529 CE, Emperor Justinian ordered the closure of all Athenian philosophical schools, which is considered the final act in the history of Ancient Athens. With the advent of Christianity, Athens lost its former status and the remnants of its former glory. Magnificent temples dedicated to the ancient Gods, such as the Parthenon and the Erechtheion on the Acropolis or the Temple of Hephaestus in the Agora of Athens, were converted into Christian churches. Many works of ancient art, including sculptures, were taken away by the Emperors of the Eastern Roman Empire (Byzantium) to their new capital Constantinople. In the subsequent years, Athens gradually transformed into a provincial town, suffering from periodic raids by Slavs and Saracens, but by the 11th century, its position stabilized, and the city began to flourish as a provincial center, far from the political intrigues and wars in which the Empire systematically participated. During this period, the abandoned ancient Athenian Agora, destroyed after the invasion of Hercules, was rebuilt, and beautiful Byzantine temples were constructed in the city, many of which have survived to this day almost in their original form. However, in 1204, during the Fourth Crusade, the Byzantine Empire, which had plunged into a severe socio-political crisis, was conquered by Frankish crusaders and fragmented into many small feudal states, one of which became the Duchy of Athens, led by the Burgundian knight Otto de la Roche. During his rule, from 1204 to 1225, defensive structures were expanded on the Acropolis, and it began to resemble more like a medieval European castle. A Gothic bell tower was added to the Parthenon,

Roman Agora in Athens in the 18th century.

which became the cathedral of the Catholic Archdiocese of Athens. A large tower appeared at the gates, which later, along with other buildings from the Crusader era, was destroyed in the late 19th century "to cleanse the Acropolis from later constructions unrelated to the ancient history of this city," despite protests from the global community. In addition, the dukes of the de la Roche family brought knightly tournaments to Athens, attracting many glory seekers from Europe who wished to join the duke's army. It is also worth noting that the Peloponnese was considered the capital of European knighthood in the 13-14th centuries, where another Crusader state was located – the Principality of Achaea, the court of the ruler of which was described as "one of the most brilliant courts of that time." After the Greeks regained Constantinople in 1261, restoring the Byzantine Empire, the Athenian Duke Guy I de la Roche became the most powerful ruler in Frankish Greece. From

1311 to 1388, the Duchy of Athens was under the rule of the Crown of Aragon, having been conquered by mercenaries of the Byzantine Emperor Andronikos II – soldiers of Aragonese, Catalan, and Balearic origin who had gone out of control. The city's history during that period is rather obscure. It is known that only Athens formed a vigueria – an administrative unit within the Kingdom of Aragon, ruled by captains and castellans on behalf of the King. In 1388, the city was wrested from the Catalans and Aragonese by the wealthy Florentine Neri (Raniero) Acciaioli – the nephew of the prominent Neapolitan politician, patron of Petrarch and Boccaccio, Count of Melfi, Malta, and Gozo, and Baron of Corinth, Niccolò Acciaioli. Conquering Athens, Neri established the last dynasty of Athenian dukes, which remained in power until 1458. Despite the duchy's economic downturn by that time, Turkish Sultan Mehmed II, upon entering Athens, was so impressed by the beauty of its ancient monuments that he issued a decree prohibiting all his subjects from plundering or defiling any buildings in the city under the penalty of death, and the Parthenon was transformed by him into the principal mosque of Athens. Since then, Athens has entered a final decline and has come to resemble more of a large village than a city. The population decreased to 20,000 people (compared to about 413,000 inhabitants in the late 4th century BCE). The Acropolis, once the castle of the dukes, was turned into the residence of the Turkish pasha with barracks and powder magazines, and the city's residents were subjected to religious persecution (especially from the second half of the 16th century). A curious incident occurred with Athens in the early 17th century when Sultan Ahmed I handed over the city to his favorite concubine – a Greek woman named Vasiliki – a native Athenian by birth. For a short period, the persecution of Christians in the town weakened. Still, after Vasiliki's death, Athens became the "income property" of the kızlar ağası –the chief eunuch guarding the harem of the Ottoman sultan. Throughout this time, the Venetian Republic – one of the largest, if not the largest, maritime powers of that time (at least in the Mediterranean), attempted to regain from the Turks the former possessions of the Crusaders and the major port cities in Greece. During one of the Venetian-Turkish wars, on September 26, 1687, Athens was bombarded by the Venetian fleet under the command of Doge Francesco Morosini. One of the shells, hitting the Parthenon directly, where the powder magazine was located, caused a powerful explosion, bringing the symbol of the ancient world to the state we can observe today. Shortly after that, Athens was briefly captured by Venice (for about two weeks), and during this time, the Venetians managed to take out of the city some valuables, including the famous Piraeus Lion, which now adorns the square in front of the Doge's Palace. During the first major anti-Turkish uprising in 1770, which was supported (both militarily and financially) by the Russian Empire, the majority of Athenians preferred to remain calm and miraculously escaped massacre after the suppression of the uprising by the Ottoman authorities. It should be noted that genocide was a common method of "punishment" used by the Turkish authorities against the Christian subjects of the sultan for their faith. One of the bloodiest periods during Turkish rule in Athens was the twenty-year reign of Pasha Hacı Ali Haseki from 1775 to 1795. As the lover of Sultan Selim III's sister and enjoying the support of the city's aristocrats, Haseki secured his appointment as the voivode responsible for tax collection in Athens. Soon, feeling his unlimited power, Hacı Ali began arbitrarily imposing new taxes, the amounts of which grew larger and larger, and reducing the allowable period for payment, allowing him to seize all the property of the "debtors" and if there was nothing left to take, to deal with their families cruelly. The situation worsened with the plague outbreak in 1789, which Haseki took no action to combat. Instead, he ordered all the orange and olive trees from the gardens of Athenians indebted to him to be uprooted and replanted in a new huge garden in front of his residence. During his rule, the population of the city decreased to a few thousand people: those who were not executed or tortured by Haseki's men and did not die of the plague or smallpox fled the city without looking back. Eventually, after the death of his mistress, Sultan Selim's sister, whose complaints against her pasha reached the ruler of the Ottoman Empire year after year, Hacı Ali was deposed, exiled to the island of Kos, and beheaded. After the start of the Greek War of Independence from 1821 to 1829, Athens changed hands several times: in 1822, they were captured by the Greek rebels, but in 1826, they again fell under the control of the Turks, under whom they remained until March 1833. Many historical monuments in Athens, mainly churches and temples, were burned and destroyed during this time. Upon the declaration of the city as the capital of the Greek Kingdom, approximately 4,000 inhabitants resided in 400 houses, primarily located around the Acropolis in the Plaka area. From that moment until today, Athens has developed as the center of the new Greek state. In 1896, Athens hosted the first modern Olympic Games at the rebuilt ancient stadium "Kalimarmaro," in the post-war period (in the 1950s and 1960s), experiencing a surge in population migration from the islands and villages, largely shaping its modern appearance. At present, the population of the Athens metropolitan area, including all suburbs, is about 4,000,000 people – almost half of the population of the entire Greece,, with about 640,000 people living in the historical Athens itself.

Day 1. Athens Center: The Face of the City.

Syntagma Square. (Exact address for Google maps: Syntagma Square). As you step onto the main square of the Greek capital – Syntagma or Syntagmatos, which translates to "Constitution Square" – the first thing you'll notice is the large palace in a restrained, neoclassical style, in front of which stands the honor guard of soldiers in distinctive uniforms familiar to many. Perhaps these soldiers are one of Athens's most recognizable "postcards." But let's go in order. The name of this square was not given randomly: the history of the Greek constitution began right here on September 3, 1843. At that time, the reigning King of Greece, Otto, was not limited by any laws in his powers and could freely dismiss the government and dissolve the Greek parliament. Moreover, the majority of the King's courtiers and closest advisors were not Greeks at all but Bavarians (the thing is, Otto was the son of King Ludwig I of Bavaria and, after his election to the throne in 1832, arrived in the country with a large Bavarian retinue). All these facts caused extreme irritation among the Greeks, especially among the veterans of the Greek War of Independence of 1821-1829 and the young officers of the Royal Army. The accumulated dissatisfaction with the autocracy of the King and the impunity of his advisors, who didn't even attempt to learn the Greek language, eventually led to an armed uprising on the night of September 2-3, 1843, as a result of which King Otto introduced the first constitution in the history of the Greek Kingdom. However, His Majesty systematically violated it, leading to his overthrow in 1862. Nevertheless, in memory of the significant date that marked the first step of the Greek state towards democracy, the square in front of the Royal Palace, where the uprising took place on September 3, 1843, was named Constitution Square.

Old Royal Palace. And now, let's take a look at the Royal Palace itself. Today, it is known as the Parliament Building or the Old Palace, as since 1935, it has been the seat of the highest legislative body of Greece, known by its ancient Greek name "Vouli" (or "Bule," according to the norms of ancient Greek pronunciation) the unicameral parliament with funds personally loaned for this construction by his father, King Ludwig I of Bavaria. Ludwig was a great admirer of antiquity and, in his small Kingdom, erected many remarkable architectural monuments, such as an exact copy of the Athenian Temple of Hephaestus and a replica of the Parthenon in full size. When his younger son, Prince Otto, was

View of the Old Royal Palace in 2024.

elected King of Greece, Ludwig, without exaggeration, was delighted and was ready to supply his son with as much money as needed to formalize his son's status properly. And how should the status of a King be formalized? Of course, with a palace., The best architects from Bavaria who prepared the construction project were sent to Athens by King Ludwig: Eduard Schaubert, Leo von Klenze, and Karl Friedrich Schinkel. The latter, by the way, proposed to build the royal palace directly on the Acropolis. Yes, on that very Acropolis, because in ancient times, it was precisely there that the Basileus (King) of Ancient Athens resided. Fortunately, this project was rejected (it was opposed by King Ludwig of Bavaria himself, considering that its implementation would destroy the historical appearance of the Acropolis), and on February 6, 1836, the construction of the palace began on the very site proposed by the architect Friedrich von Gärtner. Almost all the materials for the construction were taken from the outskirts of Athens: if you look closely, at the end of Queen Sofia Avenue, to the left of the palace, you will see a forest-covered mountain ridge. Mount Hymettus – from there, wood, stone, and marble were transported to construct the palace. Another source of materials (mostly finishing stone) was Mount Lycabettus – the highest hill within the city limits, located twenty minutes' walk from Syntagma Square. Greeks from the islands of Naxos, Tinos, Paros, and Anafi, who made up the majority of the workers, brought individual materials from the Greek islands and Italy to construct the palace. The natives of the latter island, after the completion of the construction, were granted by King Otto permission to take any plot of land they liked in Athens as a reward and to build houses for themselves from the remnants of construction materials, and that's how another landmark of Athens appeared, which we will talk about later when we approach the Acropolis. Von

King Otto I of Greece, son of King Ludwig I of Bavaria.

Gärtner's original plan called for rich neoclassical decoration on the palace's façade. Of course, all these embellishments, such as sculptures, pilasters, and stucco, required much time and money. When King Ludwig I of Bavaria saw von Gärtner's plan, he took out a red pencil. He crossed out everything he deemed unnecessary for economic reasons and because of the departure of neoclassical norms of building decoration from strict ancient traditions. In the end, only what you can see on the palace façade today remains of the décor. In response to King Ludwig's edits, the architect said:

"Well, Your Majesty... now it's truly barracks." Since the completion of construction in 1847 and until 1922, the Greek Royal Family lived in the palace. Until 1862, King Otto I and his spouse, Queen Consort Amalia. After their overthrow and the election to the throne of Greece of Prince Christian of Denmark (who ruled under the name George I), who

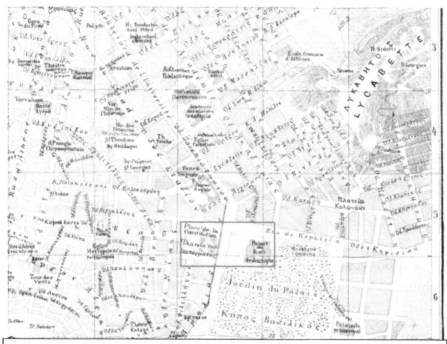

Map of the centre of Athens. In the red rectangle are Constitution Square (Syndagma) and the Old Royal Palace. The map is from 1890, but is still usable today.

founded a new dynasty, his large family resided here. The last inhabitant of the palace was the widowed Queen Olga – the spouse of George I, who left Greece after the coup in 1922. At that time, the Royal Palace was confiscated from the Royal Family and used to accommodate Greek and Armenian refugees from Turkey who were fleeing the genocide carried out by Mustafa Kemal's forces in 1921-1922. After the overthrow of the monarchy in 1924, the palace gradually deteriorated without proper maintenance until, in 1929, the government of the Second Hellenic Republic decided to move the Greek Parliament's chamber into it, which until then was located in the old building on Stadiou Street (today it houses the National Historical Museum of Greece). However, the palace was unsuitable for parliamentary sessions, and only the summer of 1934 saw the completion of its costly renovation. The Fifth National Assembly officially opened its doors on July 1, 1935. Since then, the Greek Parliament has continuously convened in this palace, despite the fact that in the same year, the monarchy was restored and King George II – the grandson of George I and Olga – ascended the throne.

Evzon Honor Guard (Evzon – from the Greek "Well girded.")
Let's look closer at the Evzones, the presidential palace guards. Their role is similar to that of the famous Grenadier Guards of Buckingham Palace. The Evzones last participated in a military conflict in 1940-1944 when an elite partisan unit was formed from the Evzones regiment, successfully operating against German, Italian, and Bulgarian forces in the mountains of occupied Greece, earning the nickname "Devil's Army" from their enemies. Nowadays, the Evzones stand guard in front of the Old Royal Palace, where the Tomb of the Unknown Soldier is located – a monument to all those who died for the freedom and independence of their homeland, Greek warriors. The central element of the composition depicts a dying hoplite — an ancient Greek, specifically Athenian, warrior. On the left and right sides of him, two phrases are carved ancient script, which can be translated as "And one bed remains empty for the unknown" and "Any land is the tomb of famous men." Beneath thes inscriptions are listed all the battles in which the Greek army participated from 1912 – the beginning of the First Balkan War – until 1922 – the end of the Secon Greco-Turkish War. Battles of the Second World War and all subsequent wars in which the Greek army participated are not included in the monument, as it was unveiled in 1929. Now, let's take a closer look at the unusual attire of the honor guard soldiers. First, let's interpret their name – "Evzones." Translated from Greek, it means "well-girt," and the term refers to their traditional attire, which today you can see on the Evzones only on state holidays and Sundays. Among other things, it is distinguished by a wide sash, in which, in the past, one could tuck several pistols and knives. Another distinctive feature of the Evzones is the brightly red cap with a long silk tassel called the "phareon." Today, this tassel is believed to symbolize the tear Christ shed on the cross, and the red color represents His blood. In reality,

however, it is more likely that the "phareon" originated from the classic Turkish headgear – the fez. The white shirt with wide sleeves, complementing the ceremonial attire of the Evzones every Sunday or on national holidays (such as March 25 or October 28), is paired with a white skirt called a "fustanella." As the elders used to say, this skirt has exactly 400 pleats – corresponding to the number of years the Greek people lived under Turkish rule. And again, my dear traveler, I must admit that this is nothing more than a beautiful legend. Indeed, there are many pleats on the fustanella, but more often than not, there are far fewer than four hundred. The Greek people did not live under the Turks for four centuries: Athens, for example, was conquered by the Ottomans in 1458, and the flag of the Greek state was raised over the Acropolis in 1828, that is, after 370 years. However, let's return to our Evzones. Unlike the "phareon," the skirt "fustanella" has more solid Greek roots. It most likely comes from the Doric chiton, which ancient Greeks in the Peloponnese wore in early ancient times. Then this chiton became the prototype of the Roman toga, a shortened version of which – the Byzantine apron "podea" – was worn by representatives of the akritoi class (from the Greek word "akri" – "border"), peasant-warriors who lived on the eastern borders of the Byzantine Empire and protected it from the raids of Central Asian barbarian nomads in the 11th-

Since its establishment in 1867, the Evzone regiment took part in the first Greco-Turkish War (1897), the first (1912-1913) and second (1913) Balkan Wars, the Greek intervention in Asia Minor (1919) and the Second Greco-Turkish War (1919-1922), in World War II (1940-1944) and in the Greek civil war (1944-1947).

15th centuries. This apron became the direct "ancestor" of the fusta-nella. The most challenging element to manufacture in the ceremonial attire of the Evzones is the elaborately embroidered vest, called a "fermeli," adorned with golden threads. Like the "phareon" cap, it likely has Eastern roots. Nevertheless, one of the types of traditional embroidery on the "fermeli" ornament contains Greek letters "Χ" and "Ο," meaning "Χριστιανός" and "Ορθόδοξος" – "Christian" and "Orthodox." Regardless of the weather, each Evzone wears two pairs of woolen socks, held by a wide leather belt hidden under the clothing. This belt additionally supports the soldier's back and, in some way, facilitates his hour-long standing guard duty. The socks are adorned with silk tassels, similar to those on the "phareon" cap. The most peculiar part of the Evzone's uniform is the bright red shoes with pom-poms, called "tsarouhia" (singular – "tsarouhi"). Their name comes from the old Turkish word "çaruk," denoting sandals with a leather sole. Here, it should be noted that the Turks, most likely, borrowed this word from Italian, where a shoe similar to the Greek "tsarouhia" is called "chiòchiera." These rigid, sturdy boots with wooden soles are made from four pieces of dense leather, and initially, similar shoes were worn by Greek peasants in mainland Greece. In those times, "tsarouhia" was worn by women and children, but the pom-poms on their footwear, unlike men's shoes, were multicolored. The Evzones' "tsarouhia" are quite massive footwear, each boot weighing about three kilograms (6.6 pounds), and their sole is studded with fifty steel nails, allowing the marching Evzones to strike the pavement impressively and not to slip on marble. I assume you've noticed how powerful the Evzones' calf muscles are. Now you know why. The height of the Evzones cannot be less than 1.87 meters (6 feet and 1 inch), and a candidate for the Presidential Guard must have a robust physique at the time of application, so the Evzones in Greece are carefully selected handsome men. On the day of the union of Greece with the island of Crete (December 1), the Evzones wear a different uniform – a traditional costume of Cretan Greeks with red breeches instead of the fustanella and a blue jacket instead of the shirt. On the day of remembrance of the Pontic Greek genocide (May 19) (Pontus – the region on the Black Sea coast of modern Turkey, where a large Greek community has lived since ancient times), along with the Evzones in traditional attire, soldiers in the attire of Pontic partisans — black, with high leather boots and traditional headgear — are also on guard duty. The change of the honor guard occurs once an hour, so be careful: you cannot approach the Evzones too closely in front of the parliament building. Suppose you want to take photos from a closer distance. In that case, I advise you to bypass the Old Royal Palace and turn onto Herodou Attikou Street, where the residences of the President and the Prime Minister of Greece are located. Evzones are also on duty in front of the presidential palace, where you can approach them more closely.

Hotel Grande Bretagne.

But let's move on and turn our gaze to the grand, elegant hotel at the intersection of Queen Sophia Avenue, King George I Street, and Panepistimiou Street (University Street). That's the Hotel Grande Bretagne —

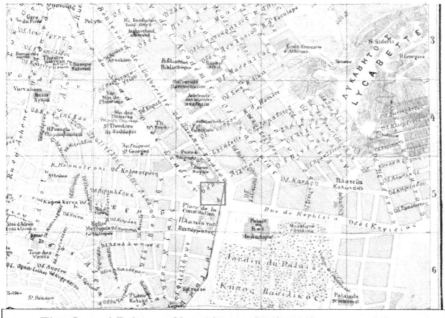

The Grand Brittany Hotel is marked on the map with a red square and the letter "b".

one of the oldest and most expensive hotels in Athens, and indeed in all of Greece. The hotel with this name originally opened in 1866, a little further down the street, at Stadium Street and Karageorgi Serbs Street. However, in 1874, the hotel moved to a building purchased from the French Archaeological School, known before that as the residence of

Andonis Dimitriou – a beautifulneoclassical mansion built by the Austrian architect of Danish Norwegian origin, Theophilus von Hansen. This name will appear several times during our journey, so keep it in mind.

The first owner of the Grande Bretagne after its relocation to the Dimitriou Palace was the Greek chef Eustathios Lampsas, who managed to make his establishment the best hotel in the Balkans and even in the entire Middle East (which Greece was occasionally considered geographically incorrectly). In 1888, this hotel became one of the first electrified buildings in Athens. Worldwide fame probably came to it after the first present Olympic

General view of the hotel and facade elements

Games, held in Athens in 1896: thousands of distinguished guests from all over Europe came to the Greek capital, and many stayed at the Grande Bretagne. Subsequently, the hotel became known for the events of December 1944 – January 1945 when the legitimate government of King George II of the Greeks returned from exile and held sessions within its walls. At that time, immediately after the lifting of the German-Italian-Bulgarian occupation of Greece, the country faced a difficult situation: the communist partisans, who had fought against the occupiers, could not find common ground with the monarchist partisans, and the nation was on the brink of civil war. Immediately after His Majesty's government returned to Athens, the city witnessed a series of heavy street battles in which the British army supported the Greek monarchists under the command of General Ronald Scobie,

View of the hotel in the 19th century

whose headquarters were also at the Grande Bretagne Hotel. Since the Greek communists believed that Sir Winston Churchill, the Prime Minister of the United Kingdom, who arrived in Athens at the same time, would also stay at the Grande Bretagne, they attempted to mine the building's foundation and blow it up along with the entire Greek government, the British command, and Churchill himself. Fortunately, this terrorist act was thwarted by a British patrol, who timely arrested the perpetrators. After the Second World War, the hotel quickly recovered and again topped the list of the best hotels in the Balkans. During the funeral of the last King of the Greeks, Constantine II, in January 2023, it was here that his royal relatives stayed: Prince and Princess of Wales, Royal Princess Anne, King of Bulgaria Simeon II, the head of the Serbian Royal House, and many others.

Henry Schliemann's Mansion **(Exact address for Google maps: Athens Numismatic Museum).** But let's leave this citadel of the rulers of the universe and head down Panepistimiou Street, away from the bustling Syntagma Square. Soon, on your right, you'll come across a large and

distinguished three-story mansion with elegant arcades. That's none

Heinrich Schliemann.

other than Henry Schliemann's Mansion, not the Trojan Palace, but the Illium Palace, as Ancient Troy was called in ancient times. But who is Henry Schliemann, and what does he have to do with the city from the Homeric epics? The connection is direct, my dear traveler: Schliemann is the man who uncovered its ruins to the world and sparked the "archaeological fever," earning him the title of the "father of field archaeology." Henry Schliemann was the son of a modest pastor from Mecklenburg. Still, at an early age, he showed multiple talents: he quickly mastered languages, knew how to turn any adversity to his advantage, and was extremely enterprising. Eventually, his desire for a better life and adventure led him first to the

Netherlands, where he successfully served in a trading company in Amsterdam, and then to Russia, where he prospered in trade, amassing a substantial fortune. In 1850, he set off for the United States of America to the goldfields of California. He returned with $60,000 in gold and continued to run his trading company, supplying the Russian Imperial Army during the Crimean War of 1853-1856. Since childhood (as he wrote, though his accounts are not entirely reliable), Schliemann had been drawn to the ancient Near East and Greek cities, especially those described by Homer: Troy and Mycenae. He had been planning an ex-

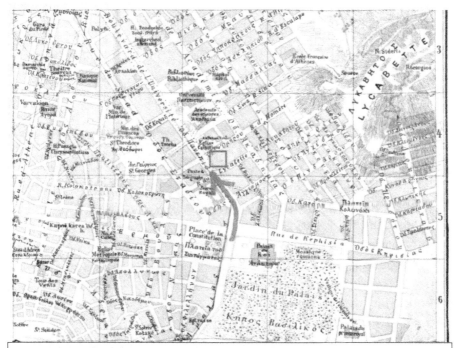

The red arrow indicates the direction of travel from Syndagma Square to Heinrich Schliemann's mansion (in the red square).

pedition to search for these cities for years, even learning Ancient and Modern Greek in preparation. In 1868, Henry Schliemann arrived in Athens. He met another amateur archaeologist and professional architect, Ernst Ziller (whose name, like that of Theophilus Hansen, you should also keep in mind, as it recurs in discussions of Athens' architectural heritage). By then, Ziller had already participated in unsuccessful attempts to find Ancient Troy. His stories prompted Schliemann to decide to go to the Troad – the region in western Turkey where, according to all the evidence from ancient and classical authors, historians, and geographers, lay the Kingdom of Troy and its magnificent capital, Pergamon, which Schliemann was eager to discover. He began his full-scale excavations on the hill of Hisarlik, beneath which, he believed, lay the ruins of Troy's capital in 1871. These excavations bore little resemblance to professional archaeology. Schliemann's hired men with shovels and picks were searching for gold, as it was supposed to be the main value of the Trojan ruins, wasn't it? They had no concept of such essential principles of modern archaeology as the cultural layer, so it is worth noting that Schliemann and his enthusiasts caused colossal damage to the ruins they discovered. Nevertheless, the 8,833 gold objects he found, dubbed by Schliemann himself the "Treasure of Priam" (without any grounds for associating it with the name of the Trojan King Priam mentioned in ancient sources, who ruled during the Trojan War), became a sensation worldwide (despite the fact that the soil layers in which the gold objects were found date back to much earlier times than those described by

Frescoes on the vaults of the terrace of the Schliemann mansion.

Homer). After Troy, Schliemann organized excavations at the site of Ancient Mycenae on the Peloponnese Peninsula, where he also discovered tombs, which he called "Royal," containing, among human remains, gold jewelry and coins weighing 13 kilograms. He groundlessly associated the gold funerary masks found by Schliemann with the Mycenaean

King Agamemnon and his family members. However, as with Troy, they belonged to earlier times than the events described in the "Iliad." Nevertheless, Henry Schliemann earned a considerable fortune from these excavations, part of which he invested in 1878 in constructing a luxurious 28-room mansion near the Royal Palace in Athens. The architect was Schliemann's friend, Ernst Ziller, and the main decorations of the building's interiors were to be Schliemann's numerous archaeological finds (mostly Trojan, as Mycenaean gold, by agreement with the Greek government, became national property as soon as it was extracted from the ground). Henry Schliemann lived in this mansion with his second wife, Athenian Sophia Engastromenos, and their two children: daughter Andromache and son Agamemnon, who would become the Greek Kingdom's ambassador to the United States and a deputy in the Greek parliament. In 1926, to cover his debts, Sophia Engastromenos, by then a widow sold the Illium Palace to the Greek government, which opened the Museum of Fine Arts in it. However, the museum did not stay in Schliemann's mansion for long, and in 1929, the Greek State Council moved in, followed by the Supreme Court in 1934, which continued to convene in the palace until 1981. Over time, the building fell into disrepair, and after 1981, it was closed. Only in 1998, after restoration work, was the Numismatic Museum exhibition housed in the mansion, which can still be seen there today.

The Catholic Cathedral of St. Dionysius the Areopagite.

The following notable structure on this street won't keep you waiting, and it will be located on the same side as the Ilion Palace. It is the Catholic Cathedral of St. Dionysius the Areopagite – the main Catholic church in Athens and the seat of the Catholic Archdiocese of Athens. Yes, Greece is an Orthodox country; moreover, Orthodoxy is specified in the Constitution of the Hellenic Republic as the state religion. All Orthodox priests are civil servants, with salaries paid from the country's budget. Nevertheless, among the Greeks, there is a small number of Catholics, the majority of whom are families of native inhabitants of the Ionian Archipelago (the islands of Corfu, Ithaca, Kefalonia, Lefkada, Zakynthos, etc.), many of which were conquered by the Kingdom of Sicily as early as 1185 and subsequently came under the rule of the Crusaders, the Republic of Genoa and Venice, the French Empire of Napoleon I, and

finally, Britain until 1864 when the Ionian Archipelago was transferred to the Kingdom of Greece. Over these nearly 700 years, the native inhabitants of the islands – the Greeks – were largely "Italianized" and

Portrait of Lysandros Kaftantzoglou (1811-1885) by Nikiforos Lytras. National Gallery of Athens.

merged into the ranks of Venetian aristocracy particularly by adopting Catholicism and creating their special dialect of the Greek language with many borrowings from Italian. In this way, the Greek Catholic community emerged, which today constitutes the majority of parishioners of this cathedral. Other parishioners include residents f Greece from Poland, Croatia, and former French colonies in Africa. The cathedral itself was founded in 1853 on a plot of land acquired jointly by the Catholic community of Athens, and the original project was drawn up by the Bavarian architect Leo von Klenze, taking as a model the main church of the Abbey of St. Boniface in the

Bavarian capital of Munich. The construction was supervised by the Greek architect Lysandros Kaftantzoglou (those of you who decide to visit the National Gallery of Art in Athens will be able to see a large portrait of Mr. Kaftantzoglou by the Greek artist Nikiforos Lytras). The construction took twelve years, and in its final stages, at the request of King Ludwig II of Bavaria (the nephew of the first King of Greece, Otto, known for his extravagant behavior and colossal spending on the construction of fairy-tale castles throughout Bavaria), the interior of the cathedral was decorated with stained glass windows by Karl de Bouché, depicting Saint Amalia, Pope Sixtus II, Telephorus, and Athanasius the Great – on the right side, and Saint Otto, Anterus, Claudius, and John Chrysostom – on the left. In 1869, during a visit to Athens, Emperor Franz Joseph I of Austria donated a significant sum to produce two marble cathedrals for this temple, which you can see to the left and right of the altar if you find the church open.

Neoclassical Trilogy. (Exact address for Google maps: National and Kapodistrian University of Athens).

Behind the Cathedral of St. Dionysius, three other architectural masterpieces await your gaze – the Athenian Trilogy. I hope you haven't forgotten the name of Theophilus von Hansen – the architect behind the building now occupied by the Grand Bretagne Hotel? Well, all these three buildings were also designed by him in collaboration with his elder brother, Hans Christian Hansen, and the first, in 1841, was the opening of what is at the center – the building of the National University of Athens (at that time called the Royal University of Otto). The project for this building was mostly the work of Hans Christian Hansen, while his younger brother Theophilus assisted in its construction – his star would rise a little later and eclipse the glory of his older brother. The University was partly funded by the personal funds of King Otto of Greece (hence its initial name). It became the first institution of higher education in the Balkan Peninsula and the eastern Mediterranean region. To this day, the National University of Athens remains one of the best in the region despite the economic difficulties of recent decades. If you approach the university building closer, you will notice a large fresco in the colonnade depicting His Majesty Otto I surrounded by muses representing various scientific disciplines: philosophy, history, archaeology, law, and others. Two marble sculptures in front of the university – monuments to Count Ioannis Kapodistrias (on the left) – President of the First Hellenic Republic (1828-1831), whose name today bears the National University of Athens, and Adamantios Korais (on the right) – one of the founders of modern literary Greek language and inventor of Katharevousa – "pure Greek language," which was a completely purified conversational Greek language with some norms

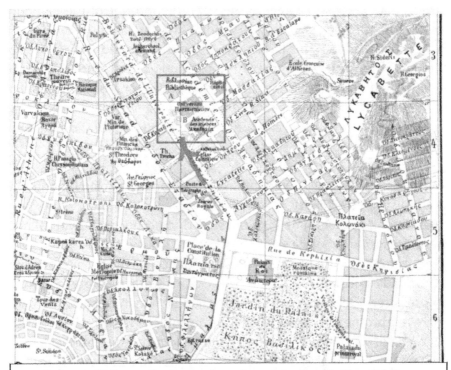

Athens Trilogy (in the red rectangle): A – National Library; B – National University; C – National Academy.

from Middle Greek (Byzantine) language. Throughout most of the history of independent Greece (from 1828 to 1976), Katharevousa was the official literary language: government decrees were published, books and school textbooks were issued, newspapers were printed, and many representatives of the Greek upper class spoke it. However, the overwhelming majority of Greeks never accepted Katharevousa as the language of everyday communication, which led to a situation in Greece similar to the Norwegian Bokmål and Nynorsk dichotomy. In

Building of the National University of Athens.

the end, artificial Katharevousa was abolished in 1976, although government decrees continued to be published until 1985.To the right of

Baron Theophilus von Hansen

the University building, the Palace of the National Academy was designed by Theophilus von Hansen in 1859, and construction began in the same year, funded mainly through donations from the Austrian banker of Greek origin, Baron Georg Simon von Sina, who later invited Hansen to Vienna. Bringing von Hansen's project to life took 28 years, with breaks in 1864-1868 and 1876. Ernst Ziller, known to us, also supervised the construction work, and the grand opening of the Academy building took place on March 20, 1887. Besides the Academy, this building housed collections of the Numismatic and Byzantine Museums for some time.

Still, since 1926, it has been entirely dedicated to the needs of science and fine arts. On two columns in front of the central pediment of the building, you can see sculptural images of the ancient Goddess Athena – the patroness of the city, and Apollo – the God of the Sun and the

Building of the National Academy of Greece.

arts. At the stairs, marble ancient philosophers sit – Socrates and Plato – some of the most famous Athenians of all time. The last, third

The building of the National Library of Greece. Monument to Panagis Vallianos right in front of the building.

building of the Athenian Trilogy is the National Library of Greece. Theophilus von Hansen also drew up its design, and construction was alsooverseen by Ernst Ziller, starting later than all the other buildings of

the Trilogy – on March 16, 1888, funded by the brothers Panagis, Marinos, and Andreas Vallianos – prominent merchants and shipowners, natives of the island of Cephalonia. In their memory, the library building became known as the "Vallianion" (the tradition of naming buildings after those who donated to their construction was widespread in Greece in the 19th century, and this tradition explains many names of architectural landmarks in Athens, for example – the Zappeion Exhibition Hall, erected with funds from the Zappas brothers). The collection of the National Library, previously housed in the building of the National University to the right, was

Ernst Ziller (1837-1923), court architect to His Majesty King George I of Greece.

Facade of the National Academy building.

transferred to this palace in 1903 and remained there until 2017, when the majority of the vastly expanded collection was moved to the new library building at the Stavros Niarchos Foundation Cultural Center.

Elements of the facade of the National Library building and the monument to Panagis Vallianos

Colonnade of the facade of the National University building.

Here, the collection's most valuable books and manuscripts are kept, and access is only possible by special permission. This library houses 4,500 Greek manuscripts – the world's most extensive collection. Among them, in particular, are the "Golden Bulls" – edicts of the Byzantine Emperors, sealed with their signature and seal, and extensive archives from the period of the Greek War of Independence 1821-1829. In front of the staircase of the National Library building, you can see a monument to Panagis Vallianos – the eldest of the Vallianos brothers, the "father of the Greek merchant fleet," whose contribution to the financing of the construction of this building was most significant. In addition, it is necessary to note Vallianos's contribution to overcoming the severe influenza epidemic in Greece that broke out in 1896. With his donation of £2,000, the Greek government managed to purchase the necessary medicines and expand the capabilities of hospitals for the admission and accommodation of patients. In 1900, he donated 200,000 Greek drachmas to peasants on the Greek islands whose farms suffered from pest invasions.

Square of Tears. (Exact address for Google maps: Klafthmonos Square)

Suppose you cross the street from the National University of Athens building and walk through a small pedestrian square with glass pyramids, which are part of the decoration of the Panepistimiou metro station. In that case, you will notice an allegorical sculpture depicting three female figures merging into one. That's Klafthmonos Square, or "Square of Tears." Don't be alarmed; there were no mass shootings or terrorist acts here, as one might assume from the name. On the contrary, the history of this place is quite comedic, but, as befits Greece, it is comedic in the style of Thucydides; that is, the irony here is quite tragic. Leo von Klenze, a Bavarian architect commissioned by King Otto I of Greece to draw up the first master plan of Athens, suggested naming this square after Aeschylus – the ancient Greek playwright known as the "father of European tragedy." However, after the first Royal Mint on this square opened, it became known as the "Mint." This name, however, did not last long: after March 25 was established by Royal decree as the day of celebration of Greece's Independence from the Ottoman Empire, and on this square, in 1838, the first festive events related to this date took place, the square itself was renamed "March 25 Square", and later – "Democracy Square." Its current name, however, emerged in 1878 at the suggestion of the

Square of Tears (indicated by a red rectangle). The red arrow indicates the direction towards it from the Athens Trilogy.

Greek journalist and writer Dimitrios Cambouroglou, who served in the Athenian newspaper "Estia." This name was associated with a

The «Estia» newspaper is one of the oldest Greek newspapers, published continuously since 1876.

remarkable fact about the political system of the Greek Kingdom in the 19th century. According to the established tradition, each new government was formed by the party that obtained the most seats in parliament during the elections —completely replaced the entire administrative apparatus, dismissing all civil servants, down to the secretaries and archivists of ministries and departments, and hiring new employees from among its supporters. Given that from 1833 to 1901, Greece had 72 governments (some of which resigned a day after being appointed), such personnel rotation occurred extremely often, and hundreds, if not thousands, of people lost their jobs. Traditionally, after their dismissal, they staged a mass protest in front of the Ministry of Economy building, which was located right on this square (it was demolished in 1940), and the new government, as a tradition, ignored them. Thus, this square was dubbed the "Square of Tears" in Cambouroglou's article. This name stuck for a long time – to this day, as well as the tradition of lower-ranking civil servants holding their protest actions on it (more precisely, next to it, at the entrance to the Ministry of Labour) at least every week.

Museum of the City of Athens. (Exact address for Google maps: Ioannou Paparrigopoulou 5-7, Athlna 105 61)

Walk down the left side of the square along Paparrigopoulou Street. You will see an elegant neoclassical three-story building on your left, adjacent to a two-story mansion of a delicate peach color. These buildings are part of the Museum of the City of Athens. In the smaller building, constructed in 1833-1834 by the German architects Lüders and Hoffer, King Otto I of Greece resided with his consort, Queen Amalia, from 1836 to 1843. This mansion was originally built for the prominent Greek entrepreneur and merchant Stamatis Dekozis Vouros, who provided it to the royal couple until the construction of the future Constitution Square Royal Palace, already known to us, was completed. Amalia, from 1836 to 1843. This mansion was originally built for the prominent Greek entrepreneur and merchant Stamatis Dekozis Vouros, who provided it to the royal couple until the construction of the future Constitution Square Royal Palace, already known to us, was completed. Since the Royal Family lived in this building for seven years, the old Athenians often called Vouros' mansion the "Old Palace." Still, now this title belongs to the parliament building. At the same time, this mansion houses a collection of furniture, accessories, and other everyday items belonging to the Athenian aristocracy of the 19th century, acquired by Stamatis Vouros' great-grandson, Lambros Eftaxios. Among the notable items in this museum are the portrait of King Ludwig I of Bavaria, the father of Greek King Otto, and one of the royal thrones used by the first

Greek monarch. Additionally, children aged 10 to 14 can have their photographs taken in exact replicas of the ceremonial attire of King Otto and Queen Amalia.

National Historical Museum.

Return to Stadiou Street and walk in the direction of the traffic flow. You will find yourself at Kolokotronis Square at the next intersection – right in front of the old building of the Greek Parliament, which now houses the National Historical Museum of Greece. In front of this building stands a large equestrian monument to Theodoros Kolokotronis – one of Greece's national heroes and the leader of the Greek War of Independence from 1821 to 1829. Kolokotronis came from a family of klephts – a particular class of Greek bandits that existed during the Ottoman rule over Greece. The klephts brazenly attacked Turkish merchants, occasionally stormed the Sultan's outposts, frequently engaged in maritime piracy, and targeted Turkish and Egyptian ships. Kolokotronis led his small band of klephts at the age of 15 and later served in the Russian Imperial and British Royal navies, but disillusioned with the prospects of Foreign Service, and he returned to his natural craft. In 1821, he rose to lead one of the major centers of anti-Turkish rebellion on the Peloponnese Peninsula. For his brilliant victories over the enemy, he was unanimously elected the ruler of the not-yet-formed Greek state at the National Congress of Greeks in Astros in 1823. Soon, however, his fiery temperament and excessive vanity alienated Kolokotronis from many other leaders of the Greek War of Independence, and the result of this quarrel was his imprisonment on the island of Hydra, from which Theodoros was released after 4 months. Towards the end of the war, Kolokotronis vigorously supported the candidacy of Count Ioannis Kapodistrias for the position of head of the Greek state. After his assassination in 1831 by members of the influential Mavromichalis clan, Kolokotronis became a member of Greece's interim government until the country's King was elected. As a politi-

Queen Consort of Greece Amalia of Oldenburg, wife of King Otto I.

cian, Kolokotronis proved to be much less capable than a military commander: his volatile temperament led to serious conflicts with other government members, and the conflicts he constantly incited ultimately almost led the country to civil war. After the election of Prince Otto of Bavaria as King of Greece, Theodoros Kolokotronis led the opposition to the new government. They were sentenced to twenty years' imprisonment in the fortress of the city of Nafplion for attempting a coup in 1834. However, a year later, Kolokotronis was pardoned by King Otto himself, reinstated to the rank of general, and awarded the Grand Cross of the highest Greek Order of the Saviour. Only after this did the "old man from Moria" (Moria – the second name of the Peloponnese Peninsula – Kolokotronis' homeland) finally reconcile with the government and spend the last six years of his life in the State Council of the Kingdom of Greece. The monument erected to him after his death points in the direction where the only prison in Athens once stood, and therefore, with the bronze Kolokotronis behind them, the Athenians joked that "Theodoros simply points to the parliamentarians where they belong." As for the old Parliament building, it was constructed not so long ago: the first session there opened only in 1875. Initially, on this site stood the mansion of Alexandros Kondostavlos – a Greek banker and politician born on the island of Chios and from an ancient aristocratic family whose lineage dates back to the Byzantine Empire.

Theodoros Kolokotronis (1770-1843).

In this mansion, from 1833 to 1835, lived the first King of Greece, Otto, who arrived in Athens, then departed to Bavaria to marry Princess Amalia of Oldenburg, who became Queen Consort of Greece after that, and upon returning to Athens, they lived in the well-known mansion of Stamatios Vouros on Paparrigopoulou Street. After the uprising on September 3, 1843, when King Otto was compelled to limit his power by the first constitution of the Greek Kingdom, the so-called National Assembly – a precursor to the modern Greek parliament – gathered in the mansion of Kondostavlos. For its needs, the large hall of the mansion was slightly modified to resemble a classical meeting hall. However, in October 1854, the old building completely burned down, and only four years later, under the guidance of Queen Consort Amalia, the construction of a new building for the Greek parliament began according to the design of the French architect François Boulanger. However, in 1859,

The building of the National Historical Museum and the monument to Theodoros Kolokotronis.

construction had to be halted due to a lack of finance. In 1862, Otto I and Amalia were overthrown and returned to Bavaria, where they spent the rest of their days, never acknowledging the fait accompli. When Prince Christian Wilhelm of Denmark was elected to the Greek throne, becoming King of the Hellenes under the name George I, a brick meeting hall was hastily erected near the unfinished building, where the parliament of the Greek Kingdom convened for the next 12 years until the construction of the building that stands before your eyes today was completed. In the final stages of construction, the Greek architect

Panagis Kalkos supervised, who was also the author of the Athens City Hall building project. During the time the Greek parliament convened in this building (from 1875 to 1932), it witnessed many important events in the history of the Greek state. Among them were Greece's bankruptcy in 1893, the First Greco-Turkish War in 1897, and the assassination of Prime Minister Theodoros Deligiannis on these very marble steps on May 31, 1905. Deligiannis, who held the position of Prime Minister of His Majesty King George I five times (he was prime minister for about five and a half years), was known as a fighter against gambling clubs, which were a real scourge then. In general, Greeks are quite fond of gambling even today. As you walk around Athens, you will surely notice many branches of the "OPAP" network – the current monopoly in gambling and betting, where local pensioners and easy money hunters can spend days on end. In those days, instead of "OPAP," there were card clubs and semi-legal casinos, where many Athenians systematically lost fortunes. The assassins of Prime Minister Deligiannis were two men: a compulsive gambler named Maniatis and a former porter and bouncer at a gambling club named Andonis Gerakaris, a father of five. Shortly before, on the initiative of Deligiannis, a law was passed that significantly restricted the activities of gambling establishments, resulting in many of them closing. Maniatis lost hope of "getting even," while the father of many children, Gerakaris, lost his only means of livelihood, which prompted them to assassinate the prime minister out of revenge. Theodoros Deligiannis died on the spot, and the murderers were apprehended, sentenced to death, and hanged in the fortress of Palamidi in

Over the 202 years of the political history of modern Greece, the country has had 176 prime ministers (not counting the 13 heads of provisional governments). At the same time, during the 1981 year of the existence of the Holy See in Rome, there were 266 Popes.

the town of Nafplion on the Peloponnese peninsula. In the same building, on March 25, 1924, the Prime Minister of Greece, Alexandros Papanastasiou, announced the overthrow of King George II and the proclamation of the Second Hellenic Republic. That marked the final stage in the history of this building as the venue for the sessions of the Greek parliament: in 1932, the highest advisory body moved to the former Royal Palace on Constitution Square, and this building, upon the proposal of Prime Minister Eleftherios Venizelos, was handed over to the care of the Historical and Ethnological Organization of Greece for the establishment of the National Historical Museum exhibition. However, at that time, neither the Historical Organization nor Greece had the financial resources to convert the building into a museum. In 1940, Greece entered a war with Italy, which, despite the decisive victory of the Greek forces, only served as a prelude to the full scale invasion of Axis powers into the small kingdom in the southern Balkans. After the German occupation of Athens began in 1941 and the collaborationist government of General Georgios Tsolakoglou came to power (one of the Greek Quislings), the old parliament building temporarily housed the Ministry of Justice, which vacated the

Prime Minister of the Kingdom of Greece Theodoros Deligiannis (1824-1905).

premises in 1943. The building was transferred to the Historical and Ethnological Organization of Greece by special decree of the prime minister with the obligation to "keep the future Historical Museum open to the public at all times." After Greece was liberated from occupation in 1944, this decree became one of the few that the collaborationist government issued that was not revoked. Nevertheless, the museum did not open, and in 1953, the city government discussed demolishing the building due to its dilapidated state and erecting several administrative buildings on its site to accommodate the secretariats and offices of the ministries of economy and internal affairs. However, a special commission of the Historical Organization of Greece, tasked with assessing the value of the old parliament building for the history of Greece, concluded that it should not be demolished. In 1961, a complete restoration was carried out. After this, on June 21, 1962, the National Historical Museum opened its doors. Its collection now includes British cannons used throughout the Greek's War of Independence from the Ottoman Empire in 1821-1829, personal belongings of Kings Otto I and George I and their consorts – Queens Amalia and Olga, as well as the writing desk and chair of the first head of independent Greece, Count Ioannis Kapodistrias, portraits of leaders of the Greek War of Independence, weapons, and clothing of Theodoros Kolokotronis, and much more worth seeing.

St. George Karitsi Church. (Exact address for Google maps: Pl. Agiou Georgiou Karitsi 5).

Continuing our journey into the depths of the old city, we turn right from the old parliament building, past the monument to Theodoros

St. George Karitsi Church.

Diligiannis killed on its steps, and come out onto Anthimiu Gazi Street. Here, we turn right again and reach the junction with Christu Lada Street, along which we turn left to Karitsi Square, adorned with the marvelous St. George Karitsi Church – named after the noble Athenian family of Kritsis, who, during the Ottoman rule over the city, founded the Church of St. George on this site, which was destroyed during the Greek War of Independence from 1821 to 1829. The church you see now was built on the old foundation from 1845 to 1849 by the already-known Greek architect Lysandros Kaftandzoglou, who supervised the construction of the Catholic Cathedral of St. Dionysius the Areopagite. This church follows Byzantine architectural canons and deviates slightly from them in some elements. The protruding bell tower of gray marble stands out from the general rhythm – a rather peculiar and unique solution for Athenian churches.

Cathedral of Athens. (**Exact address for Google maps: The Mitropoleos square).**

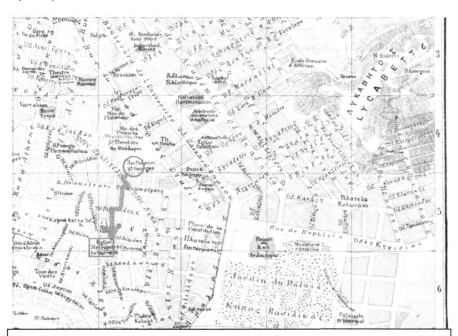

The path from the Church of St. George (indicated by a red circle) to the Metropolitan Cathedral (indicated by a red rectanle).

Now, entering the labyrinths of narrow and not always convenient streets of the old city, winding and intertwining like cracks spreading from a blow to glass, the most important thing is not to get lost. Exit onto Praxitelous Street, and when it meets Kolokotroni Street, take a slight right: you will see the entrance to the narrow Thiseos Street. Walk along without turning until you reach Pericleous Street, then turn right again onto another narrow street, Fokionos. It will lead you to Mitropoleos Square (Metropolis Square), where the main Orthodox

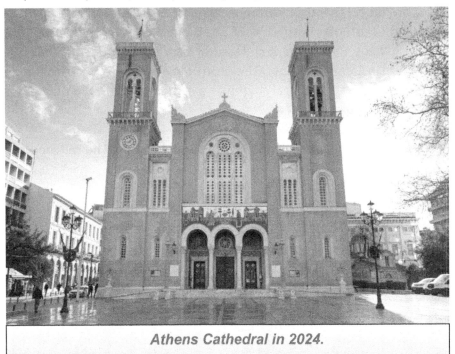

Athens Cathedral in 2024.

church of Greece is located – the Cathedral of the Annunciation of the Most Holy Theotokos, which we, Athenians, call "Mitropoli" because it is the center of the Athens Metropolis and it is here that the Archbishop of All Greece – the head of the Greek Orthodox Church – serves. This beautiful church was founded on Christmas Day, December 25, 1842, by King Otto I of Greece and his consort, Queen Amalia, with the original project by the young and already familiar to us, Theophilus Hansen. According to his project, the church was built up to the height of the first row of windows, after which 1843 work was suspended due to lack of funds. Three years later, with money donated by King Otto I from his

Wedding of Prince George of Greece and Denmark and Princess Marie Bonaparte in the Cathedral.

funds, construction was resumed by Greek architect Dimitrios Zezos, who added Byzantine motifs to the project. Still, progress was slow, and the cost exceeded the original budget. This difference was also covered by a large donation from Baron Georg Simon von Sina, familiar to us for his involvement in the creation of Hansen's Athenian Trilogy; however, work was still halted in 1857 following the death of architect Zezos. After that, the cathedral's construction was entrusted to the Frenchman François Boulanger and the Greek Panagis Kalkos – the same individuals who had contributed to the construction of the old parliament building. To expedite the completion of construction, the architects used marble taken from the destroyed Byzantine churches of Athens and its surroundings during the Greek War of Independence of 1821-1829. Finally, the cathedral was consecrated in 1862, shortly before the overthrow of Otto I and Amalia. Under the new King George I, this church became the cathedral of the Athens Metropolis and acquired its present nickname. Since then, it has hosted the most significant church ceremonies, such as weddings, baptisms, and funerals of the Greek Royal Family members, prime ministers, and later presidents of the Greek Republics (Second and current – Third). Since the exile of Otto I in 1862, no Greek monarch has been crowned, but they have undergone the enthronement ceremony in this cathedral. The last royal wedding held here was the wedding of Prince Philip of Greece and Denmark – the youngest son of the King of the Greeks Constantine II and Anne-Marie of Denmark – which took place on October 23, 2021, and was attended by many members of the ruling and non-ruling Royal Houses of Europe. The last royal funeral was that of His Majesty the King of the Greeks, Constantine II, held here on January 15, 2023; however, the coffin with the monarch's body was displayed for public farewell not in the church itself but in the chapel of St. Eleftherios next to it, which violated protocol, as according to the Constitution of Greece, the funeral of a former head of state must have state status and follow a special ceremony. Inside the Cathedral of Athens are the sarcophagi containing the relics of two particularly revered saints in modern Greece. In the right nave lie the remains of His Holiness Gregory V, the Ecumenical Patriarch of Constantinople, who was hanged by order of the Ottoman Sultan Mahmud II in response to news of the Greek uprising against Turkish rule on the Peloponnese Peninsula. Despite Gregory V not supporting the Greek rebels, fearing reprisals by the Turkish authorities against the Greek population of Constantinople (then known as Istanbul, which still had a large Greek diaspora dating back to Byzantine times), he could not avoid his fate. According to legend, the patriarch's body hung at the gates of his residence for three days before the Turks removed it and, after desecration, threw it into the sea. The body was later found by sailors of a Greek merchant ship named "Saint Nicholas" and taken to Odessa, a city with a significant Greek population at the time. It was during this time in the Russian Empire (which included Odessa at that time) that the first Jewish pogrom occurred: among the Greeks, there was a rumor that the body of Patriarch Gregory V had

Gregory V (1746-1821). Patriarch of Constantinople.

been desecrated not by the Turks but by Jews. Subsequently, the Greek residents of Odessa looted the Jewish quarter of the city, resulting in the deaths of 17 people. Eventually, the remains of Patriarch Gregory V were buried in the Trinity Church of the Greek Orthodox Church in Odessa, and they were not transferred to Athens until 1871. In the left nave, also in a sarcophagus, lie the relics of Saint Philothei, the patron saint of Athens. Philothei, born Paraskevi (Revula) Benizelou, was the only daughter of the wealthy Athenian Angelos Benizelos, who came from an ancient patrician family, and his wife Syrigi, who was related to the Palaiologos Dynasty, the last dynasty of Byzantine Emperors. Philothei was born in her father's house in Plaka, the old center of Athens, on November 21, 1522, nearly 70 years after the Turks conquered the city. Interestingly, the Benizelos family house has been restored and is now open to visitors as a museum, which we will discuss later. Since the girl was her father's only heir, Angelos Benizelos dreamed of marrying her to a noble Athenian to pass on his estate to his grandchildren. However, her only marriage was unsuc-

Saint Philothea of Athens

Below the Cathedral of Athens there is a small museum that displays Royal Thrones used during church ceremonies, ancient gospels and much more.

cessful: her husband, the Athenian patrician Andreas Hilas, was much older than his fourteen-year-old bride and died just three years after their marriage, leaving Paraskevi childless. After his death, she became a nun against her father's will and took the name Philothei. Inheriting her father's entire estate and house in the center of Athens, she used all her resources and influence to aid Christians in escaping Turkish tyranny. In her mansion, she sheltered Athenian women who were to be

Apostle Peter with keys. Detail of the carved ornament of the doors of the Cathedral of Athens.

View of the side of the Cathedral and the Church of Agios Eleftherios.

taken to the harems of wealthy Muslims or sold into slavery for disobedience, as well as Greeks fleeing from the island of Cyprus when it was conquered by the Ottomans, who had committed a terrible massacre of the island's Christian population. Additionally, Philothei founded a monastery in the northern suburb of Athens (now a district of the Greek capital) called Psichiko, where Athenians and other Greeks seeking refuge from persecution also found shelter. Her humanitarian work became so extensive that at one point, Philothei engaged in direct correspondence with the Great Council of the Republic of Venice, which had ongoing wars with the Ottoman Empire from the 15th to the 18th centuries. With the Great Council, she discussed the possibility of Venice providing financial assistance to Greeks fleeing persecution by the Turks. Naturally, such activities did not go unnoticed by the Ottoman authorities: on the night of October 2-3, 1588, Philothei was seized by janissaries in the Church of St. Andrew in Patission (now a district of Athens) and brutally beaten. She succumbed to her injuries on February 19, 1589, in her monastery in Psichiko, where sisters took her from the community she had founded. Shortly after her martyr's death, she was canonized by the Greek Orthodox Church and is revered today as the patron saint of Athens and Athenians.

The Church of St. Eleftherios.
A modest chapel lies in the shadow of the Cathedral, to its right side facing the facade. Its dome's tiles, long since faded by the sun, are now covered in grass and moss, seemingly forgotten by all. However, do not trust your eyes. Before you stands a unique example of Byzantine architecture, created almost exclusively from remnants of ancient temples, sanctuaries, and other ancient buildings. Perhaps (but not certainly), it is the last Orthodox church in Athens consecrated before the city's capture by the Frankish Crusaders in 1204 – the Church of the Virgin Mary, the Quick to Hearken to the Prayers, and St. Eleftherios. This church earned its long and intricate name not without reason: it stands on the site where, in ancient times, the sanctuary of the Goddess Ilithyia resided – one of the daughters of Hera and Zeus, and therefore a sister to Athena, whom pregnant women sought for assistance in childbirth. It is possible that the sanctuary was destroyed in the 4th century AD. In its place, some early Christian churches dedicated to the Virgin Mary were

erected, and, according to ancient tradition, pregnant women still came seeking help. In this case, the Virgin, Quick to Hearken to the Prayers, can be seen as an "adaptation" of the pagan patroness of childbirth, Ilithyia, into new Christian rituals. The dedication of the church to St. Eleftherios (one of the early Christian saints venerated in the Greek Orthodox Church, numbering seven) also likely refers to the pagan Goddess Ilithyia, whose name in Ancient Greek is etymologically related to "Eleutheria" – "Freedom," and takes forms like "Elefthusa" and "Lithiria." Based on such a close connection between the church's name and the former pagan sanctuary on its site, some historians have speculated that this

The Church of St. Eleftherios.

temple was built as early as the 7th-8th centuries AD, which is likely false, as the construction of the church involved not only marble and limestone blocks taken from the ruins of ancient buildings but also "construction materials" from clearly more recent structures, at least from the 11th-12th centuries. That led historians to suggest that the church was consecrated not long before the capture of Athens by the Crusaders in 1204 by the Orthodox Metropolitan of Athens, Michael Choniates. However, this dating is disputed by one curious detail. Walking around the church to the right of the entrance, you will notice a marble slab lying on its side in the upper part of the wall opposite the facade, covered with ancient Greek inscriptions. This slab is mentioned in the travel notes about Athens by the "father of archaeology" – the Italian

Renaissance humanist Cyriacus of Ancona (1391-1449), who wrote about it still being on the Ancient Agora of Athens in the year he visited

Farewell to King Paul in the Cathedral of Athens. March 7, 1964.

the city (1436). Therefore, it is quite likely that this church was built not only during the period of Catholic rule over Athens but also when the

Monument to Emperor Constantine XI Palaeologus on the square in front of the Cathedral.

history of the Catholic Duchy of Athens was gradually coming to an end. You can see all those various elements, which are called spolia if you closely examine the walls of the Church of St. Eleftherios. Perhaps the most remarkable among them (besides the aforementioned slab) is the long part of the Attic calendar frieze above the church entrance. This marble frieze dates back to approximately the 1st century BC. It represents a series of figures depicting the signs of the zodiac, scenes of harvesting, and elements of the Panathenaic Games (sports-religious festivals held annually (Small Panathenaea) and every four years (Great Panathenaea) in Ancient Athens in honor of the city's patron goddess – Athena). You can also notice the cross pattées placed near the frieze – there are grounds to believe that they depict the coat of arms of the de Villehardouin family – a line of Crusaders from Champagne, who ruled the Principality of Achaea (in the Peloponnese peninsula) for almost a century.

Monument to Archbishop Damaskinos.

Archbishop Damaskinos (1891-1949) during his tenure as regent of the Kingdom of Greece (1944-1946).

Opposite the Cathedral, on a marble pedestal, stands a bronze monument to the Archbishop of Athens and All Greece Damaskinos. Like many other outstanding Greeks of the 19th and 20th centuries, this remarkable individual did not come from a noble or wealthy family. He was born in a mountain village called Naupaktia, west of Attica – the region with Athens at its center. His birth name was Dimitrios Papandreou (sharing a surname with three Greek prime ministers from the same political dynasty). For ten years (from 1928 to 1938), Father Damaskinos led the Greek Orthodox Diocese in America. After the German occupation of Athens began in 1941 and the deposition of Archbishop Chrysanthus, who refused to collaborate with the collaborationist government of General Tsolakoglou, Father Damaskinos was elected as the new head of the Greek Orthodox Church. However, it should not be assumed that Damaskinos supported the Germans and members of the Greek government who sided with them. On the contrary, the new Archbishop openly stated that the racial theory of the German National Socialists contradicted the Orthodox worldview and was abhorrent to any Christian. He actively began to assist Greek Jews, whom the occupation authorities had started to arrest en masse since April 1941, sending them to death camps and forced labor. By secret order of Archbishop Damaskinos, parish priests of the Greek Orthodox Church began issuing fake baptismal certificates to Jews, which de jure made them Greeks. In some parishes, following Damaskinos's appeal, priests tried to hide Jews from the Gestapo in church basements, in their own homes, and the homes of Greek parishioners. In total, thanks to Damaskinos's actions, about 1500 people were saved from being sent to death camps. In 1970, posthumously, the Yad Vashem Institute in Israel awarded him the honorary title of Righteous Among the Nations. In addition to him, 363 citizens of Greece distinguished themselves in this field, including Princess Alice of Greece and Denmark, the mother of Prince Philip, Duke of Edinburgh, who sheltered the family of Rachel Cohen in her house in Athens.

Monument to Emperor Constantine XI.

A little further away, in the depth of the square, stands in the shade of trees a bronze monument to the last Emperor of Byzantium, Constantine XI Dragash Palaiologos. His name is associated with one of the most tragic pages in the history of the Greek people – the fall of Constantinople and the complete conquest of Byzantium by the Ottoman Turks on May 29, 1453. Although by that time, the Byzantine Empire only retained the city of Constantinople within its fortress walls and the Peloponnese Peninsula, governed by Constantine XI's younger brother, Thomas Palaiologos, the decision of Sultan Mehmed the Conqueror to finally "resolve the Christian question" and to take the capital of the last fragment of the Roman Empire by storm (it was the Romans who called their Empire that, also preferring to call themselves not Greeks or Hellenes, but Romans – Romeans) became a real catastrophe, marking the beginning of four centuries of Islamic rule over most of the ancient

Greek lands. The established tradition in Greece to be cautious of the 13th day falling on a Friday has its specificity: here, one can often hear about the fear of Tuesday the 13th. And this peculiarity is also connected with the history of the fall of Constantinople: May 29, 1453, fell on a Tuesday, and if you add up all the digits from the number 1453 (1+4+5+3), you get the number 13. As for Emperor Constantine XI, he, his younger brother Thomas, and his elder brother and predecessor on the Imperial throne, John VIII, tried their best to defend the remnants of their state, attempting to secure the support of the Pope and European powers by uniting the Orthodox and Catholic churches into one universal Christian church. For this purpose, Emperor John VIII attended the specially convened Ecumenical Council in the Italian city of Florence in 1438-1439, where a special document on the union of the two largest Christian churches was even signed – the "Union Decree." According to this document, the Emperor of Byzantium and the Patriarch of Constantinople recognized the importance of the Pope

Despite the fact that Constantine XI is most often depicted crowned, the last Emperor of Byzantium was not crowned in the traditional sense of the word: at the time of his accession to the throne, the Empire was in such a depressing situation that instead of a golden crown, a priestly hood was placed on his head.

in the united church as the successor of the Apostle Peter. They undertook to accept the Catholic tradition of worship. But this "decree" was firmly rejected by the Greek clergy and part of the Byzantine aristocracy upon Emperor John VIII's return from Italy. The Supreme Admiral of the Imperial fleet, Loukas Notaras, directly stated: "Better the Turkish turban than the papal tiara." Thus, Emperor Constantine XI, after the death of his elder brother, ascended the throne; there was nothing left but to accept with honor the fate destined for him. On the day of the fall of Constantinople, its last Christian ruler removed the signs of Imperial power and rushed into battle with the Turks who had entered the city, where he met his heroic death. This monument is an author's copy of the sculpture by Spyros Gogakis, installed in 1989 in Mystras – the last bastion of Byzantium on the Peloponnese Peninsula, a major fortress city on a cliff near Ancient Sparta. Another accurate copy of this monument is located in the port town of Piraeus, near the Church of the Holy Trinity, at the intersection of King George I Avenue and National Resistance Street, and in the Athens district of Paleo Faliro, you can see an equestrian monument to Constantine XI.

Church of the Virgin Kapnikarea.
Now, return to Mitropoleos Street and walk toward the traffic until you reach the intersection with Kapnikareas Street and turn right. You will immediately see a large, dark Byzantine church from the 11th century – the Church of the Virgin Kapnikarea, also known as the University Church because for quite a few decades, this church has been under the

The path from Metropolitan Square to the Church of Virgin of Capnicarea.

administration of the National University of Athens (the same one that was Royal and Othonian, and the main building of which was built by Hans Christian Hansen together with his talented brother Theophilus). This church is one of the oldest in Athens: it was built in the mid-11th century AD, possibly during the reign of Emperor Constantine IX Monomachus (from 1042 to 1055). Its nickname – "Kapnikarea" – probably comes from the name of the Byzantine state position – "Kapnikarios". This official was responsible for collecting the so-called "Smoke Tax" ("Kapnikos foros"), which taxed all additional chimneys in city houses. According to this version, the church was built with donations from this official. According to another version, the name comes from the nickname "smoky" of the icon of the Virgin Mary ("Kapnos" in Greek means

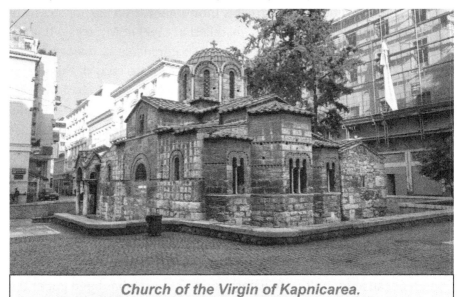

Church of the Virgin of Kapnicarea.

"smoke") and refers to the miraculous rescue of the icon of the Virgin from this church during its arson by the Turks in 1689. In either case, its name is closely associated with smoke. This temple was built on the site of an earlier church erected in the 5th century AD by the wife of the Emperor of the Eastern Roman Empire, Theodosius II, Aelia Eudocia Augusta, a native of Athens and a talented poet. Of course, her church also appeared here, but not by chance. Before it, there was an ancient sanctuary of one of the pagan goddesses (Athena or Demeter), whom many Athenians continued to worship despite its destruction by Christians. The construction of a Christian church in its place was intended to accustom the local inhabitants to worship the new, "correct God." Many elements of the temple remain in the memory of that sanctuary: parts of marble columns, steps, friezes, and four columns of different orders located in the central part of the church of the Mother of God, which you will easily find if you enter inside. During the Greek War of Independence of 1821-1829, when Athens repeatedly changed hands, this temple suffered greatly, and therefore, in 1834, the city authorities wanted to demolish it. The fate of Kapnikarea was personally intervened by King Ludwig I of Bavaria, the father of King Otto I of Greece, who allocated funds for its partial restoration. However, in 1863, the church was again slated for demolition. Still, it was saved for the second time by the direct intervention of the Metropolitan of Athens Theophilus, after which the church was handed over to the administration of the National University of Athens. The beautiful mosaic of the Virgin Mary with the infant, executed in the best traditions of Byzantine art, adorning the entrance to the Church of the Mother of God, was created in 1936 by the Greek artist Elli Vila. In 1942, one of the outstanding icon painters, Photis Kontoglou, painted a fresco of the Praying Virgin Mary inside the church.

Ermou Street.
The street where this temple stands is called Ermou – Hermes Street – and it is one of the most expensive streets in Athens in terms of renting commercial premises, but this does not mean that you cannot approach the shops and boutiques on it without being mentioned in the "Forbes" list. Not at all: prices for clothes, shoes, and accessories here can be even lower than in Athenian shopping centers, so many city residents come here during sales to replenish their wardrobe or buy Christmas gifts.

Church of St. Irene. (Exact address for Google maps: Holy Church of Saint Irene).
If you walk down this street (Ermou) to the intersection with Aeolu Street and turn right, bypassing several popular snack bars among Athenian youth, then on your right will be a sizeable neoclassical church of St. Irene – another remarkable work by the well-known Lysandros Kaftantzoglou. It was here, in the hastily restored after a devastating fire,

still, medieval Church of St. Irene, that Athens was declared the new capital of the Greek Kingdom instead of Nafplion, where the Greek government was located during the presidency of Count Kapodistrias (from 1828 to 1831). Because Count Kapodistrias was killed in Nafplion by two conspirators dissatisfied with the president's tough stance towards armed groups of klephts (former bandits), elected in 1832 to the Greek throne Prince Otto of Bavaria and his advisors – also Bavarian politicians Joseph von Armansperg, Georg von Maurer, and Carl von Abel decided to move the capital to another, yet "unblemished" city, and the choice fell on Athens – the center of ancient civilization. After Athens was proclaimed the capital of Greece in this church, it was here, in 1835, that the solemn proclamation of King Otto I as an adult and full-fledged monarch took place (when he ascended the throne, he was only 17 years old, and adulthood for monarchs at that time came at 20) and the end of the regency period. Here, in 1843, the funeral of the deceased hero of the Greek's War of Independence, Theodoros Kolokotronis, was

The arrow indicates the direction from the Church of the Virgin of Kapnicarea (in the rectangle) to the Church of St. Irene (in the circle).

held, and a solemn service was held to mark the adoption of the first constitution of the Greek Kingdom. In 1847, a decision was made to completely rebuild the historic church, which was done in the next three years under the guidance of Lysandros Kaftantzoglou, and the resulting temple combines, in addition to obvious neoclassical features, some features of Byzantine and Renaissance architecture. The first celebration held in the Church of St. Irene after the complete reconstruction was the declaration of the Greek Orthodox Church as autocephalous (self-governing) from the Patriarchate of Constantinople in 1850.

Church of Panagia Chrysospiliotissa.

Another impressive church (yes, there are very, very, very many churches in Athens) is located a bit further along our route, on the same Aeolou (Aiolou) Street, at number 60. That's the Church of Panagia Chrysospiliotissa (Virgin Mary of the Golden Cave), a name derived from the original church that stood on this site, where construction of this church began in the early 18th century with the participation of the Great Cave Monastery – the oldest Christian monastery in

Greece, built in 362, AD to com-

The arrows indicate the direction of travel from the Church of St. Irene (diamond) to the Church of Panagia Chrysospiliotissa (rectangle) and to the Krinos cafe (circle) at the end of the street, a little before reaching the Central

memorate the miraculous appearance of the Virgin's image in one of the caves on the Peloponnese peninsula, near the city of Kalavrita. The old church was burned down during the Greek's War of Independence from 1821 to 1829, and only in 1863, under the direction of the architect Panagis

Kalkos, construction of this church began, which, after Kalkos died in 1878, was completed by the famous Ernst Ziller. Thanks to him, this church represents a peculiar eclectic blend of Byzantine, neoclassical, and neo-Gothic architecture. Next to the church, a little further back, you can see the small chapel of Agia Paraskevi – a miraculously surviving structure from the era of Turkish rule, the exact founding date of which is unknown.

Café "Krynos".

Concluding our first day, I want to introduce you to one of those places that no average tour guide will tell you about and which perhaps makes many Athenians true Athenians. The "Krynos" café is a little further along this street, past the Aeolou (Aiolou) intersection with Evripidou

Café "Krynos".

Street. This excellent café, which opened its doors over a hundred years ago – in 1923 – is remarkable in that almost nothing has changed in it all this time. Since the first loukoumades (honey-dipped doughnuts) were fried in "Krynos," Greece has seen the overthrow of monarchy, its restoration, the establishment of fascist dictatorship, the repulsion of Italian invasion, occupation by Germany, civil war, restoration of monarchy again, the establishment of military dictatorship, and once again becoming a republic. Throughout all this time, an ordinary Athenian could always come to this café, order a plate of traditional loukoumades with honey and the most delicious stretched ice cream, a cup of aromatic Greek coffee with cinnamon, and briefly forget about all the madness happening beyond the large windows of "Krynos." In this café, there are no waiters: you will need to take a tray yourself and place your order at the counter in the back of the room. My recommendation – of course, the loukoumades with honey, cinnamon, and ice cream (vanilla or chocolate, according to your taste). Perhaps this is the most delicious Greek dessert you can try. You can take a glass of water for free by filling it from the tap to the right of the cash register, and then sit at any available table downstairs or on the second floor and enjoy!

Day 2. Old Athens – the soul of the city.

Monastiraki Square.

Monastiraki Square is a rather sharp contrast to the lethargic Constitution Square (Syntagmatos). Noisy, chaotic, dirty – every time I step onto it, I can't shake the feeling that I've ended up at some Eastern bazaar. Yes, it's better to come here early in the morning, when the souvenir

Now there is no roadway, but the bustle has not diminished. View of Monastiraki Square in 2024: Dzistarakis Mosque (in the center of the frame), Monastirion Station (on the right side of the frame) and the Church of the All-Holy Virgin (on the left side of the frame).

shops, tugging at tourists, are just starting to open, and all sorts of beggars and other fairground performers with bunches of laser pointers for two euros each won't stick to you every minute. There is much to see on this square, and in the gentle hour of dawn, you can have it all to yourself.

*More recently, cars drove freely around Monastiraki Square
and there was even a bus route...   (Photo from the mid-60s).*

Mosque of Tzistarakis.

Perhaps the first thing to catch your eye on this square is the nearly cubic-shaped building with four columns and a large, tiled dome. You will think it's a mosque, and wouldn't be wrong, my dear traveler. Indeed, this building once housed one of the five Athenian mosques during the Turkish rule. It was erected in 1759 by order of the Athenian pasha Cizderiyeli Mustafa Ağa, whom the Athenians called Tzistarakis, and in whose honor this mosque acquired the nickname Tzistarakis. Mustafa Ağa burned one of the Temple of Olympian Zeus columns for the construction of this mosque (according to another version – the Library of Hadrian, the ruins located right behind the mosque, making this latter version seem more likely). Some Athenians considered this act sacrilegious despite the fact that they eagerly used the ruins of ancient monuments to construct their houses and economic buildings, and we will never know how many ancient sculptures and reliefs were turned

The Dzistarakis Mosque.

Church of the All-Holy Virgin.

into lime during this time. Nevertheless, Tzistarakis' actions were reported to Sultan Mustafa III, who ordered the pasha, inclined to excessive vandalism, to be removed from his position as governor of Athens.

The mosque, however, functioned and served its direct purpose until the beginning of the Greek War of Independence from 1821 to 1829, during which (in the brief period when Greek insurgents used to control Athens) the municipal council met in the mosque building. The former mosque accommodated soldiers during dance evenings when the city became the capital of the Greek Kingdom. As a food warehouse, and after a small reconstruction in 1915, it housed the Museum of Greek Handicrafts and Folk Art exhibition. In 1975, the latter institution relocated to a new building, and the Mosque of Tzistarakis became its branch, hosting a collection of contemporary Greek ceramics until 2014. However, this exhibition has been absent from the historic building for the past ten years.

The Church of the All-Holy Virgin.
Once upon a time, during the Ottoman rule, there was a real Eastern bazaar here – large and classic for many major cities of the Ottoman Empire. It began about 100 meters (320 feet) from the square and ended here, next to the mosque. There were many taverns on the square serving specific liver snacks called "dziery," which is why this square was known among the people as "Dzlerdziidika." There were also hammam residential houses, and nearby, not far away, was the mansion of the chief tax collector – the "voivode." A little further up the street, the ruins of a madrasa – an Islamic religious school – have also been preserved, and it operated during Ottoman rule. Another name for the square in those distant years was "Stis Karotses" – "by the coachmen" – because the cab drivers constantly gathered here waiting for their clients. This square, and not Syntagma, which appeared only after the construction of the Royal Palace by Otto I, was the main square of Athens and the epicenter of urban life for almost four centuries. Its current name, "Monastiraki," is a diminutive form of the word "Monastirion" – "monastery" – and refers us to the times when almost the entire territory of this square was occupied by a monastery, which during the existence of the Duchy of Athens was male and was a dependency of the ancient monastery of Kaisariani, which is still located in the mountains of Hymettus, towering over Athens to the northeast. The main church of that monastery was the Church of the All-Holy Virgin, which you can see today opposite the mosque Dzisdaraki. This church

is quite possibly the oldest of the surviving Orthodox churches in Athens: some experts tend to date its construction to the 8th century AD, while more cautious ones – to the 10th century. The exact dating is difficult due to the large number of changes and additions that were made, mainly during the Turkish rule, and significantly altered the church's original appearance. In addition, during that period, the monastery had already become female, and how this happened is unknown

Bazaar on Monastiraki in the 18th century.

to us. But the role of the monks living in this monastery in transforming the area around it into the primary urban market is undeniable: the thick woolen fabrics sewn here were sold by the nuns themselves in small shops attached to the monastery walls. Gradually, other stalls appeared next to them: pottery, cooperage, and so on, until the monastery was "overgrown" with a bazaar. As the market expanded, the territory of the monastery decreased: the city authorities alienated its land, demolished the cells, and eventually, the monastery was dissolved entirely, and all that remained of it was its former main church, which the Athenians jokingly and seriously nicknamed "Small Monastery" or "Monastiraki" in Greek.

River Eridanus.

Now stand between the Church of the All-Holy Virgin and the Dzisdaraki Mosque and listen: if the square is quiet enough, you will easily hear

A fence behind which there is a part of a Roman sewer discovered during excavations, through which the Eridanus River flows.

Eridanus River.

the noise of water somewhere underground. Pay attention to the trapezoidal hole fenced on all sides by a fence: if you approach it closer and look down, you will see a real miracle: in a ceramic gutter, partially covered by a brick dome, at a depth of about six meters, flows a river, descended from the pages of Strabo and Pausanias, a thin stream of clear water, like a thread, connecting into a single canvas everything you see here on the surface: all the ruins, churches, hills, and mountains with that distant, almost fabulous antiquity, in which there were playwrights, philosophers, brave warriors, and Olympian Gods. That's the River Eridanus, and it flows through this pipe, passing under your feet, for 1900 years, obediently following the order of the Roman Emperor Hadrian, who wished to hide the Eridanus underground. This section was discovered by builders accidentally in 2008. Now, if you enter the Monastiraki station and go down to the blue line of the Athens metro before going onto the platform, you can come closer and behold this wonder of Roman engineering at arm's length. And if the Eridanus had not been removed into this pipe, then it is pretty likely that it would have dried up and turned into a swamp nineteen centuries ago.

Monastiraki Train Station.

Monastirion (Monastiraki) Station (green line of the Athens Metro).

And since we mentioned the metro, it's worth paying attention to. The "Monastirion" station, as it was officially called once, or "Monastiraki,"

Queen Olga (1851-1926) (born Grand Duchess Olga Konstantinovna of Russia) was so beloved by the subjects of her husband George I (who reigned for almost 50 years) that to this day the Russian female name Olga is quite common among Greeks.

as it is called now, was ceremoniously opened on May 17, 1895, in the presence of the King of the Greeks, George I, and his spouse, Queen Consort Olga. This station became an extension of the existing line "Thission-Pireaus" from 1869 – an above-ground railway with steam traction connecting Athens to the port city of Piraeus, which today, de facto, can be considered one of the districts of the expanded Greek capital. The idea of connecting Athens with Piraeus arose in the 1850s. Still, it was only in 1867 that they began to implement it under the guidance of the English engineer Edward Pickering (as is known, the English were the first to equip their capital with a metropolitan: the London Underground opened as early as 1863). Since there was nothing between Athens and Piraeus at that time except stony wilderness, there was no need to hide the railway underground, which deprived Athens of the right to call its metro the second oldest in the world. This place could be taken by the underground funicular in Constantinople, which opened in 1875. The Athens metro went underground only in 1895. With the construction of the Monastiraki station, the Omonia station was opened, which is entirely located under the square of the same name in the center of Athens. This station's interior decoration, like the Monastiraki station's elements, remained unchanged since then. However, the entire metro system was significantly reconstructed when two new, completely underground lines of the Athens metro were constructed in 1990-2004. Using one of them – the blue line – you can get from Monastiraki Square directly to Athens International Airport by purchasing a special ticket for 9 euros from a machine or at a ticket office. The journey will take 30-40 minutes if you follow the train schedule, as trains to the airport run at intervals of 35 minutes. On both sides of the station are streets of Ifestou and Pandrosu, consisting entirely of souvenir shops with various trinkets for every taste – something that still connects Monastiraki Square with its Turkish past. Opposite the station, on the roof of a relatively high building right at the corner of Ermou and Athinas streets, there is a cafe called "Roof Garden," which I cannot recommend. Still, if you want to take some good, memorable photos of the square with a beautiful view of the Acropolis, you will not be disappointed.

Hadrian's Library.

Now I invite you to follow past the Dzisdaraki Mosque up the street Areos, where we will discover a wonderful view of the only surviving part of the Roman Library of Hadrian, built in 132 AD by the order and

Ruins of Hadrian's Library in 2024.

at the personal expense of one of the greatest lovers of Ancient Greece ever to sit on the imperial throne of Rome – Publius Aelius Trajan Hadrian, known simply as Hadrian. This ruler was very different from his predecessors and many of his successors; for example, he was the only his possessions. He visited Gaul, Germany, Britain, and the Middle East

An early Christian church that existed near the wall of the former Hadrian Library, captured by daguerreotype in 1842.

during his reign. Emperor in the entire history of Rome to personally visit most of . Still, he loved Athens the most, where, in addition to the Library, he built an entire Roman district named after him – Hadrianopolis, which was separated from Ancient Athens by a wall and an arch, also preserved to our time. This Emperor also helped the Athenians complete one of the longest construction projects in the city's history – the Temple of Olympian Zeus, initiated by the tyrant Pisistratus in the mid-sixth century BC and of which only a few columns remain today. This library was magnificent: 100 by 70 meters (320 by 230 feet), with a large atrium, reading rooms, a lecture hall, and, of course, an extensive book depository, mainly containing scrolls. The library housed about 20,000 manuscripts, most of which were destroyed in 267 AD during the invasion of Athens by the Germanic-speaking barbarians of the Heruli, after which the library lay in ruins, and some parts of it were used to build a defensive wall, which the Athenians hoped would protect them from future invasions. Only in 407-412, AD was Hadrian's Library partially restored by order of the prefect of Athens, Herulius, and Christian churches soon "grew" next to it and on part of its ruins. The first appeared in the fifth century AD, and its discovery marked the transformation of the space once occupied by the library into a new market square – an economic, but at the same time, the cultural center of the now Christian Athens. Here, the first chair of the Archbishop of Athens was later established – even before it was moved to the Parthenon. Only one of those early Christian churches – built in the VI and slightly expanded and rebuilt in the VII century cruciform-domed basilica – survived until the XIX century. Joseph-Philibert Girault de Prangey captured it in one of a series of unique daguerreotypes with views of Athens, made by him in 1842. This church burned down in 1884, and in the twentieth century, the ruins of Hadrian's Library were carefully cleaned of everything unrelated to antiquity and thoroughly studied. Incidentally, it was on the library's ruins where the Athenian voivode mansion was located – responsible for collecting taxes as an Ottoman official.

Fethiye Mosque.

Portrait of Mehmed the Conqueror by Paolo Veronese.

Continuing along Dexippou Street, parallel to the fence of the Library of Hadrian, we come to another intersection where we turn right. Here, partially enclosed by a fence, stands another mosque – Fethiye. In Turkish, its name means "Conqueror's Mosque," a title held by the Ottoman Sultan Mehmed II, who won Constantinople in 1453 and ended the history of the Duchy of Athens in 1458. Upon entering the city, he ordered the construction of Athens' first mosque, naming it after his victorious title, and it is this mosque that you can see before you now. Its construction utilized the ruins of ancient buildings, a common practice in Athens, particularly in the ancient Roman Agora, where ample ruins were available. Since its opening, this mosque has operated al

Fethiye Mosque.

Monastiraki Square (indicated by a circle) and the ruins of Hadrian's Library adjacent to it lie very close to the Fethiye Mosque and the Roman Agora (indicated by a rectangle). Since 1890, in which this map was published, some of the houses on the site of the Agora have been demolished, so that the rectangle covers the modern territory of the archaeological site.

most continuously, with the only interruption occurring in the autumn of 1687 when Athens fell under the control of the Venetian Republic for just over two weeks. During this period, the Ottomans lost control, and the Fethiye Mosque was temporarily converted into the Church of St.

Dionysius the Areopagite. However, everything reverted to its previous status once the city returned to Ottoman rule. During the Greek War of Independence, when Athens was liberated from Ottoman rule by Greek rebels between 1824 and 1826, the Fethiye Mosque was converted into a school for mutual instruction where people could freely exchange skills and knowledge. In Greece during the Ottoman period, much of the population lacked formal education, and literacy was often acquired informally, typically through church or monastery schools. When Athens became the capital of the Kingdom of Greece, the former mosque served as a warehouse for flour, and in 1890, a bakery was added to it, although it was dismantled in 1935. Until 2010, the former Fethiye Mosque housed a storage facility for archaeological finds from the Roman Agora and the Acropolis. However, in 2017, after a full-scale reconstruction, the Ministry of Culture transformed it into an exhibition hall. Now, after its completion in 2017, you can enjoy a stroll through the remains of the Roman market and admire the interiors of Athens' first mosque in its original form.

The Roman Agora and the Tower of the Winds. **(Name on Google maps: Roman Agora).**

The place where the former mosque Fethiye is located is called the Roman Market or the Roman Agora – the second largest trading square in

Arch of Athena.

Athens after the ancient Athenian Agora, which the Romans arranged after capturing the city in the 1st century BC. The first Emperor of Rome,

The Roman Agora and the Tower of the Winds.

Octavian Augustus, issued the decree to build the market, as evidenced

The Tower of the Winds.

by the inscription at the entrance. It is located slightly away from the former mosque, at the intersection of Pikilis and Dioscuron streets, and there is a well-preserved arch dedicated to the goddess Athena, whom the Romans also revered, calling her Minerva. The Agora itself significantly expanded in the 2nd century AD, during the time of Emperor Hadrian; there was a stoic in addition to numerous trading stalls, shops, and workshops. One could stroll or rest in the shade at noon in this covered colonnade. Also well preserved are the remains of a Roman public toilet –

"Vespasianae." This name comes from the name of the Roman Emperor Vespasian, during whose reign (69-79 AD) street toilets were taxed, and for the first time since their appearance in the Roman Empire, they became paid. Vespasian's son, the future Emperor Titus, after the introduction of this tax, reproached his father for "taxing the latrines," to which the ruler of Rome took a coin from the bowl, raised it to his son's nose, and asked if it smelled, to which he received the answer: "non olet" – "it does not smell." "And yet this is money obtained from urine," Vespasian summed up. Since then, the famous saying "Money does not stink" – "Pecunia non olet" has spread. Another notable structure in the Roman Agora is the Tower of the Winds – the oldest meteorological monument in Athens and one of the oldest in the world. It is an octagonal tower on a pedestal with three steps, made entirely of Pentelic marble (like most marble structures and sculptures in Athens), just over 12.1 meters (39.8 feet) high, and each of its sides corresponds to a cardinal direction (North, Northeast, East, and so on). In the frieze, you can see well-preserved symbolic images of the six winds: Boreas (northern), Caecias (northeastern), Apeliotes (eastern), Eurus (southeastern), Notus (southern), Lips (southwestern), Zephyrus (western), and Skiron (northwestern). They all have their unique symbols and attributes, and looking at this tower on a windy day, depending on which side the wind was blowing from, any Athenian could understand what to expect from the weather. In addition, at the top of this tower, during its service as intended, there was a weather vane in the form of a Triton blowing into the pipe, facilitating wind recognition. Inside this tower were also water clocks (a water timer), which operated on water from underground sources with the Acropolis. The tower itself could also indicate the time to Athenians: all those houses that surround the Roman Agora today did not exist at that time, and the tower was one of the tallest structures in this part of the city, so, thanks to the lost markings around it, it acted as a sundial. This engineering marvel was a gift to the city from a certain astronomer named Andronicus of Cyrrhus (a city in Greek Macedonia), who lived in the 1st century BC. Little is known about the details of his biography. Still, the tower he gave to Athens was a masterpiece of architecture long mandatory for study by all students of art schools in Europe: it inspired the creator of the tower of the Oxford Observatory, Radcliffe James Wyatt, as well as the British engineer John Upton, who created a project for a similar tower for ventilating the book depositories of the Marine Library in Sevastopol (then – the Russian Empire, today – Ukraine).

Turkish Medrese.

A bit further from the Roman Agora, right opposite the Tower of the Winds, on the pedestrian part of Pelopida Street, among the bushes be-

The path from the Tower of the Winds on the Athens Agora (circled) to our next stop (in the rectangle) is shown by an arrow. The Musical Stairs of Plaki on Mniscleous Street will be at your right hand, as will the Melina Café, our current destinaion.

Ruins of a Turkish Medrese.

hind the benches, you can notice the remains of a certain structure with boarded-up doors. If you don't know what it is, you could easily overlook it, especially against Roman ruins. Nevertheless, this monument of Islamic architecture also deserves its "moment of fame."That's all that remains of the Turkish medrese – a spiritual Muslim school that appeared here in the 17th century and operated until Athens gained independence from the Ottoman Empire. After the city was proclaimed the capital of the Greek Kingdom by decree of King Otto I, a prison was established in the building of the former medrese, and on the branches of the ancient plane tree in its courtyard, criminals sentenced to death were hanged. This practice continued under George I until 1898, when, for archaeological excavations, most of the Ottoman architectural monuments were demolished.

"Musical Stairs" of Plaka.
Now let's turn onto Mark Aurelius Street (quite a loud name, isn't it?) and reach its intersection with Lisiou (right before the pedestrian part of Mark Aurelius Street goes up). Yes, we need Lisiou Street: it adjoins

Tables on the "Musical Stairs" of Plaka.

the famous "Musical Stairs" of Mniskleus Street – a place with its own unique atmosphere and special charm, completely occupied by taverns where live Greek music is played in the evenings. And it's not necessarily the overplayed "Sirtaki" (which, by the way, was invented only in the 1960s): on these stairs, in clubs known as "buats" (from the French word "boîte" – box), the so-called "New Wave" of Greek urban music of the 1960s was born. Many young musicians, poets, singers, and composers who didn't have the means to release their records and didn't have connections in show business made a name for themselves in

Lisiou Street.

these clubs. They later gained all-Greek fame because people from all walks of life came here for inspiration and new songs. Two of those clubs still operate today on these stairs: "Esperides" (Hesperides) and "Apanemia". About thirty such clubs were in the center of Athens (mainly in this area). I can't unequivocally recommend any of the taverns here: perhaps they have become too touristy for me lately. When such a transformation happens to traditional phenomena like Greek taverns, they lose all their appeal to me. eating in them becomes as mundane as eating at McDonald's or grabbing a bite at an airport lounge. Moreover, traditional Greek music has long been displaced in these taverns by the tourist-familiar "Sirtaki" and two or three other compositions repeated every evening from April to October.

Cafe "Melina".

Let's walk further down Lisiou Street because, besides these stairs, one of the most romantic cafes in Athens is located here – "Melina Mercouri." I can confidently recommend it to you: you won't find better crepes (thin pancakes, which came into Greek cuisine from France) with orange jam and cream anywhere else. And the mountain herbal tea (tea "vunu") they serve here! Now that's something with soul, unlike "Sirtaki" played on a bouzouki wrapped in three strings of Scotch tape. Besides, there's a whole story behind this cafe – a big and beautiful story of a Greek woman who loved her country and countries loved by this Greek woman. Melina Mercouri was one of the most famous Greek actresses of her time, if not in the entire history of Greek cinema. As Greek cinema is considered dead today, I believe it's fair to call Mercouri the greatest actress in history. She hailed from a wealthy and influential

Cafe *"Melina"*.

family: her grandfather, Spyridon Mercouris, served as the Mayor of Athens from 1899 to 1914 and from 1929 to 1934, while her father, Stamatis Mercouris, was Minister of Public Order and a member of the Greek parliament. Born in 1920, Melina (her birth name was Amalia Marina) Mercouri graduated from the National Theatre of Athens, living in Athens during the German occupation. This period in her biography was the most controversial, as she resided in a 400-square-meter (4,305-square-foot) apartment close to the Royal Palace at Syntagma Square. Despite this, she felt a bond with Greek anti-fascist partisans and actively supported the activities of the underground organization "Greek Liberation Front," coordinated by the Greek Communist Party. Through her brother Spiros, who was actively involved in resistance efforts, Melina donated substantial sums to partisan organizations, aligning closely with many Greek communists and socialists during the war, which later impacted her political career. However, after the end of World War II, particularly in the 1950s, she shone in cinema and theater. Particularly outstanding and internationally acclaimed were the films she starred in, such as "Stella" (1955), "Never on Sunday" (1960), a "Topkapi" (1964), where her co-star was the great Sir Peter Ustinov. The director of the latter two films was Jules Dassin — a film noir classic and the father of the famous French singer Joe Dassin. It was Jules who became Melina Mercouri's last life companion: they met at the Cannes Film Festival in 1955, and in the early 1960s, Dassin, an established director with a global reputation, moved to Greece to be with her. Here, he continued to create, and three of his films from this period — "Never on Sunday," "Topkapi," and "Phaedra" — each featuring Melina Mercouri, received prestigious international awards (Oscar, Cannes Film Festival's Palme d'Or, and others). After the military junta of Colonel Georgios Papadopoulos usurped power in

Melina Mercouri in her youth

the Greek Kingdom in 1967, and King Constantine II of Greece was ousted and forced into exile with his family, a large number of Greeks followed the monarch — not so much due to monarchist beliefs, but because they rejected the military dictatorship. Between 1967 and 1974 in Greece, strict censorship was introduced, all liberal and left-wing parties and movements were banned, and sometimes bizarre prohibitions were established, such as the ban on importing American popular music into Greece, which, as it seemed to the Papadopoulos government, "contradicted Orthodox Greek values." Many Greeks who left the country united in their forced emigration within strong opposition circles,

Colonel Georgios Papadopoulos (1919-1999) - head of the Black Colonels junta in 1967-1973.
The dictatorship of the "Black Colonels" in Greece lasted 7 years. To this day, it is not known for certain how exactly Papadopoulos and his associates managed to carry out a successful coup d'etat and gain a foothold in power, but the end of their regime was associated with the coup d'etat in Cyprus in 1974, the purpose of which was to annex the island to Greece, and the result was the Turkish invasion of Cyprus and its division into two parts. In domestic politics, the "Black Colonels" widely used repression against political and ideological opponents of their course: in 1969.

openly criticizing the Papadopoulos regime and calling it fascist. One such activist, and a very active one, was Melina Mercouri, who lived with Jules Dassin in Paris at the time. Her outspoken criticism of the Papadopoulos regime even led to an organized assassination attempt on her in Genoa, which, fortunately, was unsuccessful. Almost immediately after she began her activities in emigration, one of Papadopoulos's government members, Colonel Stylianos Pattakos, issued a decree stripping Melina Mercouri of her Greek citizenship. In an interview, she uttered her famous phrase: "I was born a Greek and will die a Greek, while Mr. Pattakos was born a dictator and will die a dictator." Ultimately, the junta of the "Black Colonels" isolated itself: its leaders "devoured" each other in the struggle for supreme power and failed miserably both domestically and internationally. After their regime fell, most political emigrants returned to Greece, including Melina Mercouri and Jules Dassin, after which, in the late 1970s, Melina ended her career in cinema and theatre. Her name resounded much louder among former leftist emigrants, so when she joined the Panhellenic Socialist Movement, she served in the Greek parliament for 17 years (from 1977 to 1994) and in the governments of Prime Minister

Andreas Papandreou (from 1981 to 1989 and 1993 to 1994), she held the position of Minister of Culture and Science of the Third Hellenic Re-

Melina Mercouri and David Bowie.

public, becoming the first woman to hold this position in the country's history. This café, named in her honour, was opened by her close friend, Mr. Andreas Marzaklis, who told me the story of this beautiful establishment. During Melina's tenure as Minister of Culture, Mr. Marzaklis served in the Prime Minister's residence – the "Megaron Maximou" – and thus met Mrs. Mercouri. Shortly before her death, when she was already ill, but no one suspected how serious it was, Mr. Marzaklis asked her directly: "Madam Minister, may I open a café in your honor when you are no longer with us?" to which Melina, astonished by such frankness, promised to throw Mr. Marzaklis out of the window for such questions. After she died in 1994 from lung cancer (Melina Mercouri smoked a lot), her brother Spyros personally permitted Andreas Marzaklis to open the café in memory of his sister. He helped furnish it with photographs from the actress and minister's archive. In the corner of the room, you'll see a small buffet with a collection of porcelain – it once stood in Melina Mercouri's office in Piraeus, and these little cups and saucers were especially dear to her heart – some of these items were inherited from her beloved grandfather, Spyridon. On the walls, you'll see Salvador Dali, Aristotle Onassis, Maria Callas, Jules Dassin, Robert

Kennedy, and many others – friends and acquaintances of Melina Mercouri, a woman born Greek and died Greek.

Diogenes Gymnasium.

Ruins of the Diogenes Gymnasium.

If you walk down Erechtheos pedestrian street from the "Melina" café, you'll almost immediately find yourself near the site of archaeological excavations. It is quite possible that the ancient Greek gymnasium of Diogenes was located here, but not the Diogenes with a torch in the Athenian Agora searching for a man in broad daylight and living in a large wine jar, but Diogenes of Macedon one of the great Athenian benefactors of the 3rd century BC, on whose funds this gymnasium was opened. Little is known about the gymnasium itself, but only boys were taught there, and they celebrated a festival in honor of the gymnasium's founder – "Diogeneia," during which ritual libations were made, and two bulls were sacrificed a fairly classic program for ancient festivities.

Benizelos Mansion.

Immediately after these excavations, there is an aristocratic mansion, and you may think it is built in some Moorish or Middle Eastern style. But it will only seem to you so: this style is quite Byzantine, and the mansion itself, at the back of which the presumed ruins of the gymnasium are located, once belonged to the Benizelos family, whom we got

Benizelos Mansion.

Risalit (protruding part of the facade) of the Benizelos house and courtyard.

a born cquainted with in detail while standing in front of the Athens Cathedral on Mitropoleos Square. It was here that Saint Philothea of Athens, born cquainted with in detail while standing in front of the

Athens Cathedral on Mitropoleos Square. It was here that Saint Philothea of Athens, born Paraskevi Benizelu, was born, raised, and lived most of her life, sheltering fleeing Athenian women and saving them

Interior of the Benizelos house.

Entrance to the Benizelos House Museum from Adrianou Street.

from the genocide of Greeks from Cyprus by the Turks. After her murder by the Turks, the mansion passed to one of her distant relatives, was resold many times, and by the 19th century, it was turned into a three-apartment house and divided among three families of modest means. Such families mainly inhabited the old city in those days: they had small farms in their backyards, raised chickens, sheep, and goats, and never imagined what lay beneath their feet. Unlike all other houses of the Ottoman period, this mansion was bought out and underwent careful and meticulous restoration, and after it was entrusted to the Greek Orthodox Church, a free museum operates in it, the entrance to which is located on Adrianou Street.

Sir Richard Church's House.

Now I suggest you walk along Kyristou Street (and if you visited the Benizelos House, then walk to the intersection of Adrianou and Flessa Streets and turn right) until you see a pedestrian street, usually quite deserted, called Scholiou (Scholeiou). At the end of this street, a large house with its lower part mercilessly covered in graffiti cuts across it with its empty corner. That's one of the few houses from the Ottoman period in Athens that have survived to this day in its original form. However, what interests us is not this but the fact that Sir Richard Church, a British officer, a veteran of the Napoleonic Wars, and the commander-in-chief of the Greek land forces during the final stage of the Greek War of Independence from 1821 to

Sir Richard Church (1784-1873), commander-in-chief of the Greek land forces.

1829, lived in this house. Church was born in Cork, Ireland, then part of the United Kingdom, and joined the army at 16, fleeing from his parental home in 1800. Under Lieutenant General Sir Ralph Abercrombie's command, the Church participated in the Battle of Abukir in 1801, fought in the war in Sicily, and the invasion of Naples. From 1811 to 1814, he formed and led the Greek Regiment of the Duke of York, which operated against the French in the Ionian Islands. During this time, Church earned a reputation as a phil-

Another Bonaparte.
In addition to Irish officers and English poets, among the volunteers from Europe who decided to help the Greeks win independence for their ancient homeland from the Turks, there was also a place for Paul Marie Bonaparte, Napoleon's own nephew. Paul Marie fled his home in Italy, dropping out of university to volunteer for the British Navy and fight the Turks for Greece in 1827. However, this Bonaparte did not have to become a glorious successor to his dynasty: just four months after arriving in Greece, Paul Marie accidentally shot himself while cleaning his pistol.

hellene, a "friend of the Greeks," despite advocating for the Ionian Islands to remain under the British flag after the war with Napoleon ended. Church became good friends with Theodoros Kolokotronis, whom we are already familiar with, during his service on the islands, and this fact also played a role in the Briton's election as the commander of the Greek land forces in 1827. By then, Greek military leaders had formed a permanent and power-holding interim government. One of Richard Church's first major successes in his new position was assisting Georgios Karaiskakis, one of the Greek military leaders, who attempted, along with his men, to break the Turkish siege of the Acropolis of Athens from the military camp in Phaleron, the present-day coastal district of Greater Athens. Despite Karaiskakis's death in this unsuccess-ful operation, Church gathered the Greeks scattered along the coast and transported the army to the island of Salamis, which the insurgents already controlled. Two years later, thanks to the successful command of Richard Church and Admiral Francis Hastings, the Greek forces managed to capture the cities of Messolonghi, Vonitsa, and Etoliko – three major centers in Western Greece, allowing them to control the Ambracian Gulf and thus determine the future northwestern border of Greece. For his services to the young country, Sir Richard Church (who had previously received the Order of the Bath and the Royal Guelphic Order from the King of Great Britain) became a Grand Officer of the Greek Order of the Savior and, during the reign of King Otto I, held the position of Inspector General of His Majesty's Army as a general, and later became a lifelong member of the State Council. In Athens, he initially lived in the mansion of British Admiral Sir Poultney Malcolm, who commanded the British fleet in the Mediterranean from 1828 to 1831 and later moved to a house in the center of Athens, in the Plaka district, purchased from another Briton – historian George Finlay. That's the same house that is now before us. The Turks built it in the 17th cen-tury, and, for a certain period, served as a police prison. However, the house was later completely rebuilt, and by the time Church bought it, it

Sir Richard Church's house (at the end of the street)

was a beautiful mansion where the brave Irishman lived for almost 40 years. Here, the elderly commander-in-chief was often visited by King George I, who last stayed with Church a few days before his death on March 20, 1873.

The Church of Saint Nicholas Rangavas. (Name on Google maps: Holy Church of Saint Nicholas Rangavas)

From the house of Sir Richard Church, a small pedestrian street called Epicharmou leads us to the intersection with Tripodon Street. Crossing it and ascending the stairs, we find ourselves in front of another excellent example of Byzantine church architecture – the Church of Saint Nicholas Rangavas. Like many other churches in Greece, the last part of its name – "Rangavas" – has no relation to Saint Nicholas. Still, it indicates the family who commissioned and financed the construction of this church. The Rangavas family is one of the oldest noble houses of Byzantium, from which Emperor Michael I (770-844 AD) originated. According to one hypothesis, he was the patron of this church, but more likely, this theory is incorrect. Based on all architectural evidence, the Church of Saint Nicholas cannot be

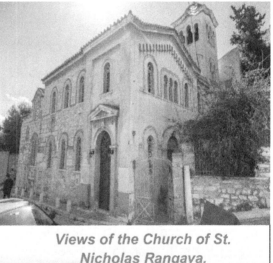

Views of the Church of St. Nicholas Rangava.

older than the 11th century. Therefore, it is more probable that it was "gifted" to the city by a younger member of the dynasty – Leon Rangavas; a commemorative inscription of whom was discovered on the colonnade of the dome during restoration works in the 1970s. The history of this church is intriguing: originally almost cubic, a cross-domed basilica, it suffered greatly during the bombardment of Athens by the Venetians in September 1687 (a wall collapsed). The boundary between the old 11th-century body of the church and the newer extension, elongating the church to the east and ending in a later neoclassical addition from the 1830s, is visible. This last addition was made during restoration works under King Otto I, during which the church was repainted. Unfortunately, the original Byzantine frescoes did not survive until Athens was liberated. This church is also notable because its bells were the first to announce to the Athenians with their loud peals the end of 400 years of Ottoman rule on Greek soil.

Anafiotika.

If you walk past this church along Pritaniou Street and immediately after the stairs, which will be on your right, turn left into a small alley adorned with graffiti, and walk through it, climbing higher and higher on narrow

Church of St. Simeon in Anafiotika. 1917.

stairs (or if you type "Anafiotika" in Google maps), you will find yourself in one of the secret places of the old city. It is secret because it magically transports you from the bustling Athens to one of the fairy-tale islets of the Aegean Sea. This village, called "Anafiotika," was built by one of the groups of workers who were invited to Athens by King Otto I from the islands of the Cyclades archipelago (Paros, Naxos, Milos, Anafi) to work on numerous construction projects, including the Royal Palace on Constitution Square. Its construction was illegal, practically piratical, and

began under the cover of night. The thing is that originally, immigrants from the island of Anafi, like other labor emigrants from the islands, were settled on the plain, in the present center of the city, near the Church of the Lifegiving Spring, not far from the modern Academias Street, where they were offered to settle with their families, building their own houses on the small plots of land allocated to them. Soon, however, land and house prices in the city began to skyrocket. The land given by the King to the islanders was not enough, so two builders from among the immigrants from the island of Anafi (according to some data, these were carpenter Damigos and mason Sigalas), along with a number of helpers, without permission from the authorities, built two huts in one night on the northwestern slope of the Acropolis in a traditional island style. They were best at building such houses because the islands of the Cyclades archipelago are mostly bare rocks, much like the Acropolis. When residents of nearby neighborhoods noticed the strange buildings on the hillside, a complaint was filed with the Athens City Hall requesting an inspection. However, when the complaint reached the

Stairs in Anafiotika.

relevant official, other islanders followed the example of the first two. The spontaneous village of Anafiotika began to grow. In·no time, King Otto I was overthrown. In the ensuing chaos of powerlessness, the residents of Anafi quickly finished their work, taking root on the slope of the Acropolis properly: now there was a real island village here. The new King of the Greeks, George I, turned a blind eye to this small but charming piracy, so Anafiotika became a new attraction in Athens. In 1922, its national composition was slightly diluted when, to the east of the village, a similarly spontaneous camp of Greek refugees from Turkey appeared, fleeing the genocide committed by Mustafa Kemal's forces.

Nevertheless, the 65 residents who live in the village today are predominantly descendants of those same builders from the island of Anafi. Their 45 houses (about 3/5 of the original village size, as in the 1950s and 1980s, it was partially demolished for archaeological excavations) range in size from 8 to 35 square meters (from 86.1 to 376.7 square feet) and all of them are cultural heritage monuments. The history of Anafiotika is not exhausted by its anecdotal origin: there is also a heroic

Manolis Glezos (left) and Apostolos Santas.

page in its chronicle. From here, on the night of May 31, 1941, two nineteen-year-old youths, Manolis Glezos and Apostolos Santas, began their ascent to the top of the Acropolis. Their goal was to remove from the flagpole in front of the Parthenon the flag of Nazi Germany, which had been raised over Athens shortly before by the occupying German forces in April of the same year. The young men managed to slip past the guards and, resorting to a diversionary maneuver, lower the flag with the swastika and tear it into small pieces, after which they descended back down to Anafiotika almost unnoticed. This symbolic act was widely covered in the world media, and General Charles de Gaulle later called Manolis Glezos "the first partisan of the Second World War." This step by Greek anti-fascists was seen as a call to action, after which a full-scale partisan war against the German-Bulgarian-Italian occupiers unfolded in Athens and other major cities, as well as in the mountains and forests throughout Greece, continuing until the country was liberated entirely in 1944. The Gestapo and the police of the collaborationist government of Greece wanted Glezos and Santas themselves. Still, Glezos was arrested only in 1942: he was imprisoned, tortured, and contracted tuberculosis, but eventually was released from prison and continued his struggle in the communist underground, where his younger brother, Nikos Glezos, fought and was arrested and executed in May 1944. At that time, Manolis himself was in prison (for the third time during the occupation), from which he managed to escape only in September 1944. At the end of the Second World War, Manolis Glezos was an active member of radical leftist movements and was repeatedly arrested and even sentenced to prison terms on suspicion of spying for Soviet Russia. But the fame of the "first partisan of the Second World War" always came to his aid, rallying Greek and global public opinion in defense of Glezos. Eventually, the Greek government recognized his contributions to the country, elevating him to Grand Officer of the Order of the Phoenix in 1997. In March 2020, at the age of 97, Manolis Glezos lost his final battle to the coronavirus infection at the Evangelismos Hospital in Athens.

Bar "Vrettos" ("Brettos").
Now, exiting Anafiotika, let's descend Stratonos Street, where the famous Acropolis cats often roam in packs, begging visitors to the "Cave of the Acropolis" taverna for a piece of grilled chicken or kebab. Right in front of this tavern, let's turn left, but be attentive: at the junction, keep to the far left – Tespidos Street. Descend it, past the old houses and gardens, via a wide staircase, through the intersection with Tripodon Street, and the next one – with Adrianou Street, after which our Tespidos Street transforms into Kidathineon Street – "Brave Athenians." Right at the beginning, on the right-hand side, you'll find the famous bar "Vrettos," attracting attention with hundreds of colorful bottles, shimmering brightly lit on shelves and forming a whole wall widthwise. This bar is part of one of the oldest distilleries in Athens, opened by Michail Vrettos in 1909 in this building on the ground floor of a historic mansion in the old town. Here, Mr. Vrettos began experimenting

The path from Anafiotika (in a circle) to the Vrettos bar (in a square). Yes, this card was issued 16 years before the bar opened. And who would have thought then that 134 years later it would be so useful?

with various liqueur flavors, offering Athenians classic mint and cherry liqueurs as well as previously unseen citrus and mastiha flavors, drawing on ancient family blending recipes from the best distilleries of the city of Smyrna (now Izmir) – one of the wealthiest Greek cities in the Mediterranean, destroyed by the Turks in 1922. As demand for Michail Vrettos's liqueurs grew, he had to expand and relocate his distillery outside the city, and since then, the bar has occupied this premises. In addition to traditional Greek drinks such as ouzo and tsipouro, in this bar, you can taste a variety of Greek wines, as well as unique mastiha liqueur and, of course, the real King of Greek brandies – "Metaxa." For those who do not consume alcohol (like myself), this bar serves the most delicious non-alcoholic mojito – the best thing to have on a summer evening in Athens.

The Paparrigopoulos Mansion.

Not every Athenian knows what is remarkable about this abandoned mansion.

Proceed a bit further along Kidathineon Street, after the intersection with Geronta Street, right in front of the souvenir shop with "ancient Greek clothing" behind the rusty fence chained with a chain. You will see the leaning, fading ancient mansion – the mansion of Ioannis Paparrigopoulos. The most attentive among you will remember this surname – the street named in his honor houses the City Museum of Athens, where, even before the museum, King Otto I and his spouse, Amalia, lived for some time. But who was Ioannis Paparrigopoulos? He was, as it should be, an interested person, and it was not for nothing that this half-ruined mansion attracted our attention. Its owner was born on the island of Naxos, and his original surname was Linardos. However, he took their surname after Ioannis Linardos was adopted by the wealthy merchant family Paparrigopoulos. Thanks to this family, he had the opportunity to study in Constantinople, where there was still a sizeable Greek community at the end of the 18th century. Like most descendants of wealthy Greek families then, he continued his education in Russia – at the Moscow Imperial University, where he studied law and the Russian language. After that, he lived in Rome for some time, studying medicine. Upon completing his education, he entered the diplomatic service, which determined his life. Since Greece did not exist at that time (early 19th century), Paparrigopoulos was accepted as a secretary of the consulate of the Russian Empire in Patras, thus becoming a diplomat of a foreign state in his homeland. In this city, he actively collaborated with agents of the secret Greek patriotic organization "Filiki Eteria" – "Friendly Company." Based in St. Petersburg, this organization admitted all Greeks and philhellenes sympathetic to the cause of liberating Greece from Ottoman rule and who had the opportunity to contribute to the armed struggle of the Greek people for their independence. The future president of Greece led the organization, Count Ioannis Kapodistrias, who served as Minister of Foreign Affairs of the Russian Empire from 1816 to 1822. Ioannis Paparrigopoulos was sent to St. Petersburg with a message from the Greeks of the Peloponnese to coordinate joint actions between "Filiki Eteria" and the inhabitants of the autonomous part of the Ottoman Empire – the Peloponnese peninsula, the abode of Greek pirates and brigands-klefts. It can be boldly stated that it was thanks to Paparrigopoulos's actions, persuading one of the key members of "Filiki Eteria," Alexandros Ypsilantis, to raise an anti-Turkish uprising in Moldavia "to divert attention," that the Greeks in the Peloponnese gained an advantage and caught the Turks by surprise, launching a full-scale uprising in March 1821. Paparrigopoulos himself returned to Greece and actively participated in the war. After its end, he became the first Consul General of the Russian Empire in the Kingdom of Greece and settled here, in this house in Athens. And it was here, on December 25, 1843, that the first Christmas tree in the history of Greece was lit – a thing previously unknown to the Greeks (on Christmas, Greeks always used

Ioannis Paparrigopoulos (1780-1874).

to display beautiful wooden sailing ships on their windows, as a symbol of remembrance for fishermen lost at sea, who would never join their families at the festive table). The Protestant German custom, unfamiliar to King Otto of Greece, a former Catholic, could have been adopted by Ioannis Paparrigopoulos as a curious, fashionable novelty from one of his acquaintances in St. Petersburg – Count Alexander Kushelev-Bezborodko, who, in turn, could have seen the first Christmas trees at the court of the Russian Emperor Nicholas I, whose wife, Alexandra, was the daughter of the Prussian King. It is believed that she introduced this tradition to Russia. It is interesting that Count Alexander Kushelev-Bezborodko was also an acquaintance and student of Count Ioannis Kapodistrias.

Street of Tripodon and the Monument of Lysicrates.

If you walk back to the Street of Tripodon (back along Kidathineon

Monument of Lysicrates.

Street, where we came from) and continue downhill, passing by one of the best ice cream cafes in the city – "DaVinci" – then immediately after it, you will notice an ancient monument resembling a narrow and tall rotunda of columns, covered with a dome-shaped roof. That's the Monument of Lysicrates – one of the masterpieces of ancient Athens, along with the already familiar Tower of the Winds, which inspired many European sculptors and architects of the XVIII-XIX centuries. It is important to note that the Street of Tripodon is one of the oldest streets in Athens, which has not changed its

104

direction, at least since the 4th century BCE: ancient buildings were demolished, new ones were built on their foundations, then Roman ones, which were then replaced by Byzantine ones, and they, in turn, were replaced by Ottoman ones, until the street finally acquired its present appearance, but just as the ancient Greek writer and geographer of the 2nd century CE Pausanias walked along this road and saw the Monument of Lysicrates, so we walk along Tripodon Street and see this very sculpture with you. Isn't it mesmerizing? As for the monument itself, it was erected in 334 BCE in honor of a wealthy Athenian named Lysicrates and was intended to remind other Athenians that this very Lysicrates was the sponsor of the best and most beautiful theatrical production of that season, which took place in the Dionysus Theatre on the Acropolis and won first place in the theatrical competition dedicated to this merry God of wine and soulful entertainments, whom the Romans called Bacchus. For winning the theatrical competition, sponsors of the performances were awarded special symbolic prizes – bronze tripods. Lysicrates received such a prize, but he decided to immortalize his victory specially and ordered a luxurious pedestal for his prize in the form of this marble-tuff rotunda, on top of which, on a stone acanthus flower, chained to it with bronze chains, the very tripod was installed. This well-preserved and unique rotunda inspired several British masters to create similar monuments in Staffordshire, in the Shugborough garden and Alton Towers park, and another copy of the Lysicrates Monument crowns the tower of St. Giles' Church in Elgin, Scotland. A copy of the Lysicrates Rotunda can also be found in the United States, where it can be seen atop the Civil War Memorial in Connecticut.

Vironos Street.The street we find ourselves on now, Vironos Street, is named, strangely enough, after George Gordon Byron, the 6th Baron Byron, the famous British romantic poet and one of the most famous philhellenes. "Viron" is a result of a direct transliteration of the surname "Byron" into Greek, that is, the recording of his English surname with Greek letters coinciding in writing but not in sound, and "Vironos" is the word "Viron" in the genitive case. It should be noted that in Athenian toponymy, Lord Byron's name is encountered with enviable frequency: I live in the Viron area, where Byron has two monuments installed in his honor and after whom a square is named, and Vironos streets are found in many suburban areas of Greater Athens. In addition, I have two Greek acquaintances named Viron, who is named, of course, after Lord Byron. This British poet gained such wide popularity amongGreeks not by chance: in 1821, after negotiations with the English Committee of Friends of the Greeks, Byron decided to move to Greece, which was

George Gordon Byron (1788-1824).

fighting for its independence. By that time, he was already too saturated with his fame, which had come to him after the publication of "Childe Harold's Pilgrimage," and at his own expense bought and equipped with supplies and weapons a whole brig, on which he hired one and a half thousand volunteer soldiers, with whom he arrived in the Greek city of Messolonghi in 1823. What he saw on the land of Hellas could not fail to sadden him: almost as much as the struggle for the independence of his home-

land, Greek military leaders were engaged in a battle with each other for power in a state not yet created by them, and Byron decided to take on the role of "arbiter" and made considerable efforts to reconcile various political groups of Greeks and unite them into one national movement. To further support their cause, Byron ordered the sale of all his real estate in England, and he slept on a campaign cot, which is now exhibited on the second floor of the National Historical Museum of Athens in the old parliament building. Lord Byron died after a prolonged illness on April 19, 1824, in Messolonghi, without seeing the long-awaited hour of freedom for his beloved Greece, about which his last words were spoken: "My sister! My child!.. poor Greece!.. I have given her my time, fortune, health!.. now I give her life!"

The Monument to Ioannis Makriyannis.

Walking down this noisy street named after Byron, past souvenir shops and cafes, we find ourselves next to the bronze monument to Ioannis Makriyannis – one of the leaders of the Greek War of Independence of 1821-1829 and possibly the most honest of all Greek military leaders of that time. Makriyannis (whose original surname was Triantafyllou, and this nickname, meaning "Tall Ioannis," was adopted later) was or-

Ioannis Makriyannis (1797-1864) was perhaps one of the most re-markable heroes of the Greek War of Independence, distinguished throughout his life for his honesty and integrity.

phaned at an early age and was given to be raised by a wealthy family in the town of Livadia, northwest of Athens. In this family, the boy was subjected to ridi-cule and physical punish-ment. He essentially be-came a servant, but the harsh conditions did not break his character: at the age of 14, in 1811, he es-caped from the foster home and entered the service as an assistant to Mr. Lidorakis – a Greek secretary to the Turkish ruler of the Epirus region, Ali Pasha. While learning the trade, Ma-kriyannis began to earn his modest capital and, show-ing himself in commerce, managed, by 1820, to accu-mulate 40,000 piastres, be-coming one of the wealthi-est Greeks in Arta (the town where he lived at that time). From the same year, he became a member of the secret patriotic organization "Filiki Eteria" and, with the start of hostilities, led a small detachment of insurgents, with whom he participated in the liberation of Arta from the Turks. After the liberation of Athens in 1822, he was appointed responsible for maintaining public

order in the city. Makriyannis managed to quickly and effectively suppress the beginning of looting and violence by Greek insurgents against residents in Athens. Still, the most heroic page in Makriyannis's biography was an exploit comparable to the feat of the soldiers of King Leonidas at Thermopylae. In June 1825, leading a detachment of 300 insurgents, he heroically defended the mills near Argos during the advance of Ibrahim Pasha's six-thousand-strong army. The Greeks managed to repel the attack and force the Turks to retreat, but they could not save Argos itself from being burned by the Muslims. Nevertheless, in that battle, Makriyannis and his warriors showed the Turkish command that they should not expect an easy victory in the Peloponnese. After that battle, Ioannis Makriyannis married an Athenian aristocrat named Katerina Skuze, with whom he had 12 children, and since then, his life has been inseparably linked with Athens. In the final stage of the war, in 1827, he participated in the heroic defense of Piraeus against the Turkish-Egyptian troops. Before the war's end, in 1828, Makriyannis was appointed by Count Capodistrias as the first president of Greece, heading the executive authority on the Peloponnese peninsula. The biggest flaw of Makriyannis as a politician was his honesty and straightforwardness, constantly making him the target of attacks and repression by various Greek rulers. His quarrel with Count Capodistrias began when the count's government demanded that all veterans of the War of Independence sign a special act pledging their full loyalty to the authorities of Greece. Makriyannis considered this requirement humiliating. Nevertheless, Makriyannis vehemently condemned the murder of

King Otto I shortly before his overthrow in 1862.

Capodistrias in 1831 but, not deviating from his principles, continued to oppose the government, demanding the introduction of a democratic constitution to limit bureaucratic arbitrariness. Similarly, Makriyannis opposed the government in the early years of King Otto I's reign. There was no place in the new Royal Army for old veterans who had won Greece's independence with their blood and found themselves without a livelihood. In 1843, Makriyannis was one of the main leaders of the officer uprising, demanding the introduction of a constitution and limiting royal power: his liberal views were well known at court, which is why the day before the officers' uprising, surveillance was set up outside Makriyannis's house. The result of this uprising was the adoption of the first democratic constitution in the Kingdom of Greece, in the development of which Ioannis Makriyannis, elected to the constitutional assembly from Athens, took an active part (in memory of this, a portrait of Makriyannis was depicted on the reverse side of the 50-drachma coin of the 1994 sample). However, soon after adopting the constitution, King Otto I began to violate it systematically, and for his participation in the uprising of 1843, Makriyannis could not escape punishment. At some point, His Majesty demanded that the brave warrior come to the palace and apologize to the King for his participation in the rebellion, to which Makriyannis replied briefly, "I am not a slave." Eventually, in 1852, he was falsely accused of plotting a conspiracy to assassinate the King and overthrow the monarchy and was sentenced to death, which was later commuted to life imprisonment. Completely false testimonies were presented as evidence, and the court's chairman was Makriyannis's enemy – Kitsos Tzavelas. Under his influence, five out of six judges voted for the death penalty, but King Otto I "leniently pardoned the conspirator." Fortunately, two years later, in 1854, the Minister of War of Greece became a friend of Makriyannis, Dimitrios Kallergis, who was able to use his influence to secure the early release of the wrongfully convicted. His last 12 years were spent in Athens, suffering from the mental disorder that had afflicted him during his imprisonment (possibly also a result of severe injuries sustained during the war). Ioannis Makriyannis suffered from hallucinations, but this did not prevent him from being elected to the new constitutional assembly in 1862 following Otto I's exile from the country. He passed away on April 27, 1864, in his home in Athens, just a week after being posthumously awarded the honorary general title for his services to his beloved homeland. By the way, Ioannis Makriyannis was a friend and frequent guest of Ioannis Paparrigopoulos, and he was the first to see the first Christmas tree in Greece at his house. "Very well, Mr. Ioannis..." he said then, "...But I still do not allow trees to grow inside my rooms."

Makriyanni and Dionysiou Areopagitou Streets.

The street facing the bronze Ioannis Makriyannis is named after him and leads to the district also bearing his name. Once upon a time, a tram line ran along it (until 1908 – a horse-drawn one, and later – an electric one), connecting the district of Academia (where the well-known Neoclassical Trilogy of Hansen from the University, Academy, and Library is located) with the coastal district of Faliro. Part of the old tram tracks can still be embedded in the pavement along the edge of noisy cafes and restaurants lined with a lush garland. Perpendicular to Makriyanni Street runs the long pedestrian boulevard of Dionysius Areopagitou, named in memory of the first Athenian to embrace Christianity after the preaching of the Apostle Paul on the Areopagus Hill and probably

Dionysiou Areopagitou Street.

becoming the first bishop of Athens. Some also tend to identify Dionysius Areopagitou with Saint Denis of Paris – one of the most revered saints of France, who lived in the 3rd century (about 200 years after Dionysius Areopagitou), but this opinion is highly debatable. So, let's continue our journey along this beautiful boulevard amidst street musicians and singers, with a magnificent view of the Acropolis, the entrance to which, by the way, is also located here – to our right, a little further from the Makriyannis monument. I will not tell you about Athens' main attraction on these pages for natural reasons: climbing the "Sacred Rock," as Athenians also call the Acropolis, requires dedicatinga whole day in your schedule, and the quickest description of this place needs to be allocated to a separate chapter. For this reason, a guide to the museums of Athens will be published by me separately.

The New Acropolis Museum.

To our left will be the huge, glass-and-concrete building of the new Acropolis Museum, standing on numerous piles, carefully driven amidst the ruins of Ancient Athens, which were discovered on the site when the builders started digging the foundation pit – a widespread cause of cancellations, postponements, and delays in construction in our city. The first museum preserving archaeological finds made during professional researchers' study of the Acropolis opened in 1874, directly behind the Parthenon. Still, as the number of artifacts increased, their storage and display needed more and more space. In addition, the Greek government's desire to return the so-called "Elgin Marbles" to Athens also dictated the need to build a modern building to house

Acropolis artifacts. This story, which became the cause of periodic tensions in diplomatic relations between Greece and Britain, began at least 30 years before Greece appeared. Throughout Ottoman rule over Athens, the Acropolis was used by the city authorities for various purposes: a mosque was arranged in the Parthenon, a powder magazine in the Erechtheion; in the medieval buildings erected under the Athenian dukes, barracks and administrative buildings were located, and for some time, a Turkish ruler of Athens lived on the Acropolis. Later (especially after 1687, when the Parthenon was blown up), the Acropolis was subjected to systematic looting, both by the Turkish authorities, who

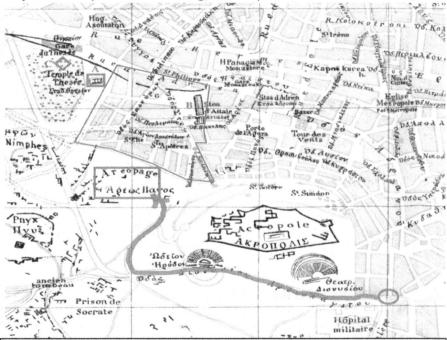

The path from the monument to Ioannis Makriyannis (circle) along Dionysios Areopagite Street, past the Odeon of Herodes Atticus to Areopagus Hill (rectangle). The ancient Athens Agora is highlighted separately on this map, because at the time when this map was published (1890), a residential area of the city was still located on the site of the Agora.
The letter A and a square mark the temple of Hephaestus; the letter B marks the Stoa of Attalus; The letter C and a diamond mark the Athens Observatory.

by then saw nothing precious in the remains of ancient masterpieces, and by the Athenians, who were not averse to burning ancient columns and sculptures for lime to build houses and using marble fragments

The New Acropolis Museum.

Thomas Bruce, 7th Earl of Elgin (1766-1841).

from ancient temples to pave roads. Thus, by the beginning of the 19th century, a huge part of the architectural heritage of the ancient Acropolis had been irretrievably lost, from which we can now find no trace. At that time (1799), Thomas Bruce, the 7th Earl of Elgin and 11th Earl of Kincardine (1766-1841), became the new British ambassador to Constantinople. Lord Elgin, like many British aristocrats of that time, was passionately interested in antiquity. From the very first days of his new appointment, he intended to compile an extensive album and collect a collection of plaster casts of various sculptures, reliefs, and other "curiosities" in the Ottoman Empire, with the authorities' permission. At that time, Britain greatly influenced the Sultan's policy. The legal side of the issue was quickly resolved, attracted primarily by the legendary Athenian Acropolis. Lord Elgin received permission for any work on copying and sketching architectural and sculptural monuments on the "Sacred Rock" and to "take any pieces of stone with old inscriptions or drawings on them." It should be noted that this document is known to us only in an Italian translation from Turkish, kept in the British Museum, and there is still debate about the authenticity of this permission. Nevertheless, upon arrival in Athens, Lord Elgin found the ruins of the Acropolis in a rather depressing state: the remains of ancient monuments were shamelessly plundered by various people, from collectors to local shepherds, who used these priceless treasures as building materials for their dwellings.

Constantine II of Greece (1940-2023) In fact, he ruled the country from 1964 to 1967. After a failed counter-coup and an attempt to regain power, the King was forced to leave Greece.

At the suggestion of his chaplain, Philip Hunt, Lord Elgin, whose initial plans did not include the removal of marble from Athens at all, decided to evacuate precious parts of the Acropolis with the help of hired Greek workers, including details of the blown-up Parthenon: half of the frieze, fifteen metopes, and seventeen fragments of pedimental sculptures. It took Lord Elgin 10 years (from 1802 to 1812) to export 200 crates of ancient marble from Greece. One of the ships carrying the valuable cargo sank in 1804 off the coast of the island of Antikythera, and only in 1806, with great effort, it was possible to raise its cargo from the bottom. For some time, this entire huge collection of antiquities was exhibited in Lord Elgin's house, after which, in 1817, it was entrusted to the British Museum, for which Thomas Bruce received compensation of £75,000, not covering even a fraction of the expenses he incurred in moving all these artifacts to Britain. Since then, the "Elgin Marbles" have been exhibited in the British Museum in London, and it can be safely assumed that at least some of these artifacts could have been irretrievably lost during the years of the Greek War of Independence of 1821-1829 if the Athenians had not ground them into building materials. So, Thomas Bruce should be considered a saviour of ancient masterpieces rather than an "unprincipled thief of Greek national property," as he is often portrayed nowadays. This very new Acropolis Museum opened in 2009, was intended to show Britain that the time had come to return these artifacts to Greece: especially for them, the museum halls feature deliberately empty pedestals, unmistakably hinting to visitors at the "debt" of the United Kingdom regarding the "Elgin Marbles." However, there can be no talk of their return "home" now: this issue was closed by the British Ministry of Culture after a series of diplomatic scandals. The first of them was related to the refusal of Greece's current Prime Minister Mitsotakis to organize state funerals for the deposed King of the Greeks, Constantine II in 1974, who was a cousin to the current King of the United Kingdom Charles III and also the godfather of the Prince of Wales. As the funerals of Constantine II were held privately, King Charles III could not attend them personally, which caused dissatisfaction in the British Foreign Office. Ten months after this unsightly incident, in November 2023, the same Prime Minister Mitsotakis, during his interview with the BBC while visiting London, stated that the "Elgin Marbles" belonged to Greece and were "stolen," likening it to "cutting half of the Mona Lisa." Mitsotakis said that shortly before meeting Sunak, the office of the British Prime Minister canceled his meeting with the Greek Prime Minister. As a Greek historian, I cannot support either side of this conflict: in my opinion, the governments of both countries behave like little children. If someday they mature for an adult, substantive, and balanced dialogue and find some solution to their mutual claims, we will all be better off. But hopes for this are slim.

Odeon of Herodes Atticus.

Continuing along Dionysius Areopagite Street, we will soon see on our right the remains of a Roman cistern for water and, right after it – a wide marble staircase, climbing which we will find ourselves in front of

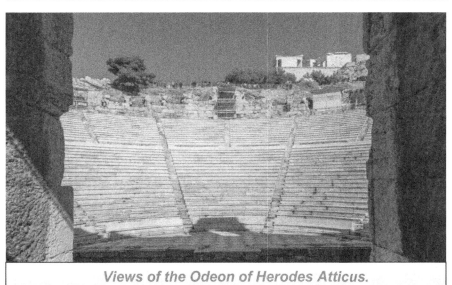

Views of the Odeon of Herodes Atticus.

the Odeon of Herodes Atticus – one of the two theatres in Greece still in operation today. It was built in 165, AD by a man with a long name:

Lucius Vibullius Hipparchus Tiberius Claudius Atticus Herodes of Marathon, or simply – Herodes Atticus. Besides being the first Roman consul of Greek descent and tracing his lineage back to the famous King Theseus – the Minotaur's conqueror and the founder of Athens Cecrops, Herodes Atticus was fabulously wealthy. In addition to funding the construction of this music theatre – the "Odeon" – the need for which arose after the collapse of the ceiling of the old Agrippa conservatory on the

Richard Strauss at the Herodes Atticus Theater in 1926.

Athenian Agora, Herodes Atticus also allocated funds for the construction of the stadium in Del phi, the Panathenaic Stadium in Athens (which, after restoration in the 19th century AD, hosted the first Olympic Games of the modern era in 1896), and many other famous ancient monuments. Herodes Atticus dedicated this theatre to the memory of his deceased wife, Rigilla, who died just before the start of construction. In 267-268 AD, 100 years after its opening, the theatre suffered greatly during a raid by the Heruli, who burned Athens. In Byzantine times, the remains of the Odeon were incorporated into the city's fortifications and, by the 16th century, became completely unrecognizable, so European travelers visiting Athens mistook them for the palace of Miltiades, an ancient bridge, and Aristotle's school. Only after Greece gained independence from the Ottoman Empire and the start of archaeological excavations on the ruins of the Odeon in 1849 did it become clear that 1700 years ago, there was a large ancient theatre here. In 1867, its stage hosted the first performance in many centuries, dedicated to the Queen Consort of the Greeks Olga, the daughter of the Russian Grand Duke Constantine and the granddaughter of the Emperor of All Russia Nicholas I, who married King George I of the Greeks and gave birth to the new Greek Royal Family. In 1920, on this stage, a year and a half before his death, the French composer Camille Saint-Saëns gave a concert, and in 1926, Richard Strauss performed three concerts here. But the Odeon came to life only after a full-scale restoration in the 1950s. After that, it acquired new, intact tribunes and lighting, and since then, it has hosted performances by world-class stars. Maria Callas, Frank Sinatra, Sting, Montserrat Caballé, and Elton John have performed here. By the way, Maria Callas is still not far from the Odeon of Herodes Atticus: opposite it, on Dionysius Areopagite Street, frozen in a bronze monument.

Areopagus.
As we conclude our day, let's walk along the winding paths leading from the Herod Atticus Theatre up to the exit of the Acropolis, where the

Areopagus Hill.

Areopagus is located –where Athenian democ racy arguably originated. Its name directly translates from Ancient Greek as the "Hill of Ares," because according to legend, it was here that the Olympian gods judged

Pericles delivers a funeral oration on the Areopagus. Painting by Philipp von Volz, 1852.

the god of war, Ares, for the killing of Poseidon's son, Alirrhotios. Since ancient times, a council of elders convened here, its members elected for life from among former archons (from the 7th century BCE, archons, who were the highest-ranking officials of Ancient Athens, were appointed for only one year). Until 462 BCE, the Areopagus elders wielded extensive judicial, regulatory, and religious authority, and it was closely associated with the emergence and development of Athenian aristocracy, as we discussed earlier. After the reforms carried out in 462 BCE by the ancient Athenian statesman Ephialtes (not to be confused with another Ephialtes, who betrayed the army of Spartan King Leonidas at Thermopylae), only the Supreme Court powers remained with the Areopagus, primarily dealing with criminal and religious offenses. As the highest judicial body, the Areopagus functioned until the 5th century BCE, after which it was disbanded and abolished. However, to this day, the Supreme Court of Greece is called the Areopagus. A memorial plaque near the ancient and now closed staircase leading to the top of the hill proclaims that here, in 51 CE, the Apostle Paul delivered a sermon. Still, this claim is disputed: most likely, during those times, the Areopagus as a judicial body convened not on the hill of the same name but in the Royal Stoa (basilica) on the Athenian Agora. Speaking of which, this ancient marketplace will be well visible from the hill of the Areopagus.

Athenian Agora.

Just under a century ago, before 1931, the site of the ancient Athenian Agora was a reasonably densely populated area of Athens. Numerous residential houses, utility buildings, and shops were gradually erected

"Vrisaki" is a district that grew up on the site of the Athens Agora in the Middle Ages and existed until the 1930s.

on the site of the abandoned ancient marketplace, starting from the time of the Crusaders (13th century). By the beginning of the 20th century, this large triangular piece of land was no different in terms of population density from the old city we walked through earlier, and, of course, the families living in this area for generations had no idea what lay beneath their old houses. The authorities of Athens, together with the American School for Classical Studies in Athens (ASCSA), which, one might say, "won the tender" for excavations at the Athenian Agora as early as 1925, in exchange for financial assistance to the government of the Second Hellenic Republic in accommodating tens thousands of refugees from Asia Minor (the peninsula now occupied by the Republic of Turkey), informed them about it. For Americans, who consider their country the first democratic state of modern times, it was crucially im-

View of the Stoa of Attalus from the Areopagus Hill.

portant to conduct excavations at the Athenian Agora – the essential part of Ancient Athens – the first democratic state in history. And for Greek officials (as usual), more preoccupied with the struggle for supreme power than with the questions of the national economy lying in ruins after a devastating defeat in the war with the Turks, money was needed to cover at least some of the population's needs. The task of the American archaeologists was complicated by just one small detail: about 100,000 people lived in the area of the Athenian Agora, occupying, according to various estimates, from 5,000 to 10,000 houses. All these people had to be resettled, and the structures obstructing the excavations, of course, demolished (and I will remind you that in 1925, about 1.2 million Christian refugees of Greek and Armenian origin, fleeing the genocide of the Christian population in Turkey, arrived in Greece, and all these people needed to be provided with shelter). As you understand, the plan of the American School was more than ambitious. Its implementation was almost thwarted by the stock market collapse of 1929 and the following Great Depression. Still, in 1931, the excavations found an influential sponsor – John Davison Rockefeller Jr., who allocated $1,000,000 for the project. Thanks to this substantial donation, 365 houses were painlessly resettled and demolished over the remaining eight pre-war years, clearing an area of 160,000 square meters (1,722,226 square feet). By 1940, under the leadership of Thomas Leslie Shear and his wife, Josephine Platter Shear, many important discoveries were made, including a previously unknown type of Athenian coin from the 2nd century BCE. In 1940, with the beginning of the German occupation of Athens, excavations on the Agora, for understandable reasons, were not conducted. They were resumed only in 1946, under the direction of Canadian archaeologist Homer Armstrong Thompson. He was the initiator of the reconstruction of the huge ancient Stoa of Attalos, the original form of which had already been sufficiently documented by archaeologists, and the well-preserved original part of the wall provided an idea of its proper height. This covered colonnade (or rather, its unrecovered original) was donated to the city of Athens in 150 BCE by the Pergamene King Attalos II

John D. Rockefeller with his son, John D. Rockefeller Jr.

as a token of gratitude for the years he spent in Athens studying under the ancient philosopher Carneades (by the way, it was Attalus II who founded and named the city of Antalya, which today is one of the largest cities in Turkey). In 267 BCE, the barbarian Heruli destroyed the Stoa of Attalos, and its remnants were used to construct the city wall. According to Thompson's proposal, all the archaeological finds on the Agora during the excavations were to be exhibited in the reconstructed Stoa. The length of the colonnade was 115 meters, the width was 20 meters (377 by 60 feet), and the cost of its reconstruction was estimated at a whopping 2,000,000 US dollars. Once again, John D. Rockefeller Jr. came to the aid of the archaeologists, allocating another $1,000,000 to the American School, after which work began without delay. What you see now is a relatively accurate copy of the ancient Stoa, slightly adapted

The rights to conduct archaeological excavations throughout the 19th and 20th centuries were one of the Greek exports: the government sold the rights to conduct research in ancient ruins for grants, certain diplomatic benefits, and so on. Thus, in 1875, the Greek government reserved the right to conduct excavations in Ancient Olympia exclusively to German archaeologists. In 1936, on the eve of the Olympic Games in Berlin, the third stage of excavations at Olympia was carried out under the leadership of the Ahnenerbe (an organization under the SS involved in creating a mythical history of the Aryan race for propaganda purposes).

for the needs of the archaeological museum, opened on September 3, 1956, in the presence of the King of the Greeks, Paul I (the grandson of George I and Olga), Queen Consort Frederica, and the Arch bishop of Athens and All Greece. Two years before this, trees began to be planted on the site of the completed archaeological work: the first two (oak and oleander) were, as expected, planted by Their Majesties, after which 654 trees and 2800 bushes were planted on the excavated Agora, which now forms the landscape of this beautiful place. Closest to us, sitting on the hill of the Areopagus, you can see the only non-ancient building preserved in this part of the city—the Byzantine Church of the Holy Apostles, built on the Agora in the 10th century on the foundation of the ancient Nymphaeum, the sanctuary of the nymphs. This church, which

View of the Temple of Hephaestus and the Acropolis of Athens from the other side of the railway (green line of the Athens metro). This postcard was issued in 1890, at the same time as the map we use.

has frescoes from the 17th century preserved in its interior, begins the Athenian style of Byzantine church architecture, which will manifest itself in the familiar churches of Panagia Kapnikarea, Saint Nicholas Rangavas, and others. On the left side, you can see the beautifully preserved ancient temple of Hephaestus — the God of Smithing. Before the excavations on the Agora, it was commonly believed that this temple was dedicated to Theseus, Ares, and Heracles. Still, inscriptions inside the temple refuted this claim and allowed it to be precisely associated with the cult of Hephaestus. It was built in the mid-5th century BCE and is perhaps one of the best-preserved ancient temples in the city. That's largely due to its conversion into the Christian Church of Saint George (most likely in the 7th century CE). Among the Athenians, this church was known by the nickname "Acamatis," and the origin of this epithet is not definitively established. According to one curious hypothesis, the word comes from the ancient Greek epithet "akamaton" in the phrase "akamaton pir" – "unquenchable fire." This phrase often accompanied descriptions of Hephaestus, known as the God of Smithing,

Temple of Hephaestus in 2024.

Church of the Holy Apostles (circa 10th century AD).

embodying the element of fire. According to a slightly comical version, the word "Acamatis" is a direct indication that the Church of Saint George in the ancient temple of Hephaestus was "lazy" ("akamatis" is one of the synonyms for "argoscholos" – "lazy"). This may be related to the fact that the Church of Saint George was open only one day a year during Turkish rule – on the feast day of Saint George the Victorious. In any case, even under the Turks, this church continued to function as a Christian church, and the last liturgy was held in it on February 2, 1833, the day of the arrival in Athens of Otto I, the newly elected King of Greece. One of Otto's first decrees was to close the church in the ancient temple, and from 1835 to 1934, it housed an archaeological museum (until 1874, the Temple of Hephaestus was the main building of the Central Archaeological Museum, which is now located on Patission Avenue). Only after the start of excavations on the Athenian Agora was the Temple of Hephaestus recognized as an independent monument, which is now accessible for visitation in that capacity.

View of the Athens Observatory from Areopagus Hill.

The Athens National Observatory.

The Athens National Observatory stands further on the hill of the Nymphs, past the Temple of Hephaestus, another creation by our friend Theophilus von Hansen. It was built over the course of four years with funding from the Austrian banker of Greek origin, Baron Georg Simon Sina, whom we're already familiar with. He also donated the most advanced astronomical equipment of that time (1846) to the observatory, and since then, this observatory has remained at the forefront of mapping Greece. There is also one of Greece's first telescopes located there – the "Doridis Telescope," which is 9 meters long and weighs 9 tons, installed in the meteorological building of the observatory in 1902. With that, we conclude our extensive walk through the old city – the heart of Athens – and will meet again tomorrow on our third day.

Day Three. What's left behind us, and what's above us.

Melina Mercouri Monument.

Here we are again, "by the shore" on Queen Amalia Avenue, next to the

Melina Mercouri Monument.

marble bust of our acquaintance from yesterday, Melina Mercouri, in the café named after her, where they serve such delicious pancakes. On the other side of the avenue stands a tempting Roman arch... Let's not waste any time and cross the road to get a closer look!

Hadrian's Arch.

This arch was erected here In 131-132 AD. It was likely part of the wall that separated Ancient Athens from the Roman "new" district called Adrianoupolis, built during the reign of the Roman Emperor Hadrian around the completed Temple of Olympian Zeus. Standing 18 meters (59 feet) tall, this arch has inscriptions in ancient Greek on its friezes (above the openings), which are now quite difficult to distinguish from the ground. If you had lived in Athens during the time of Emperor Hadrian, facing the Acropolis, you would have read: "This is the city of Hadrian, not of Theseus."

The Hadrian's Arch.

On the other side, which is not very convenient to stand on due to the bustling traffic on Queen Amalia Avenue, you would have been able to read the opposite: "This is Athens, the ancient city of Theseus." Mirac-

Inscription on the arch.

ulously, this arch survived both the invasion of the Heruli in 267 AD and the raid of the Visigoths in 396, AD, enduring the following fifteen centuries without significant damage, even after the ancient wall disappeared. Only in 1778, during the reign of the well-known "humanism" Hacı Ali Haseki, the Arch of Hadrian again became part of a wall – this time a Turkish defensive wall intended to protect Athens from Albanian brigands. The events of 1821-1829 did not affect this monument of Roman architecture either. In the mid-20th century, it finally became an independent monument when excavations were conducted around the arch, clearing the adjacent area of the remnants of Turkish walls. In recent years, however, the arch has significantly suffered from air pollution: the marble irreversibly changes color, darkening and obscuring the inscriptions under the patina. One can only hope that the Greek government will finally persuade Athenians to switch to bicycles by imposing additional taxes on petroleum products and raising fuel prices (just kidding).

Temple of Olympian Zeus.

Beyond the fence, the scaffoldings – the Temple of Olympian Zeus columns – are visible. The unfortunate temple was conceived as the largest cult building in the world (at least in Ancient Greece), and for a brief

Ruins of the Temple of Olympian Zeus in the 1880s.

period, it was. It was started during the tyranny of Pisistratus at the end of the 6th century BC, and, according to legend, this place was previously the sanctuary of Deucalion – the mythical ancestor of the Greek people, whose name is associated with the "Deucalion Flood" (its plot almost entirely coincides with the biblical "Great Flood," with the only difference being that the main characters were not Jews, but ancient Greeks and Olympian Gods). However, almost immediately after the sons of Pisistratus were overthrown, the famous commander Themistocles ordered parts of the unfinished Temple of Zeus to be dismantled to complete the construction of a defensive wall connecting Athens to the port city of Piraeus to the south. The temple was only revisited in 175 BC when the ruler of the Hellenistic state of the Seleucids (in the territory of present-day Syria), Antiochus IV Epiphanes, known for his persecution of Jews in his subject Judea (the present-day territories of Israel), considered it a matter of honor to complete the construction of the largest temple dedicated to the supreme God of Olympus. But he didn't finish it either: with the death of Antiochus IV in 164 BC, the temple was forgotten again, this time for almost 300 years, until the reign of Emperor Hadrian. The solemn opening of the completed colossal Temple of Olympian Zeus culminated the Panhellenic celebrations in 132 AD, 650 years after its construction began. This grand structure exceeded the Parthenon in size, measuring 96 meters in length and 40

Ruins of the Temple of Olympian Zeus.

meters in width (314 by 131 feet). However, as you understand, it did not last long. In 267, AD, the Germanic-speaking Heruli, who made a devastating raid on Athens, made superhuman efforts to destroy the Temple of Zeus. Although they did not raze it to the ground, the Empire had no money for its full restoration. In such a semi-ruined state, this sanctuary stood until the end of the 4th – beginning of the 5th centuries AD, when the Eastern Roman Emperor Theodosius declared Christianity the state religion in his empire, after which, for several centuries, the remains of the Temple of Zeus were used for the construction of

Christian churches and defensive structures. Ultimately, we can see the remaining parts, which were not put into construction materials, while only the foundations of the once surrounding Roman quarter of Adrianoupolis remain.

Monument to Alexander the Great.

If we proceed along Queen Amalia Avenue towards Constitution Square (Syntagma), we will soon come across the monument to

Monuments to Alexander the Great and Lord Byron.

Alexander the Great. Yes, I am ready to bet that many of you have been anticipating encountering a sculptural representation of one of the most famous Greeks in history (perhaps on par with Plato and Leonidas). It must be said, of course, that the ancient King of Macedonia, Alexander III, better known to us by the creative pseudonym "the Great," has almost no connection to Athens: it was Alexander's father, King Philip II, who had a brief war with this city, while the world conqueror himself was more focused on other parts of the Oecumene. However, an exciting and telling story is associated with this monument. Its author, Yannis Pappas, one of the most prominent Greek sculptors of the 20th century, first presented it at an exhibition at the National Gallery in 1992. At that exhibition, the museum's management proposed that the Athens municipality install this monument in one of the city squares. The proposal was accepted, and a special commission began to select the best location for its installation. Over the next 27 years, various officials, from the secretary of the Athens municipality to the Minister of Culture of Greece, could not install this unfortunate bronze monument. During this time, six mayors of Athens and ten prime ministers were replaced, while Alexander the Great continued to wait for his moment somewhere in museum storage. It is no coincidence that he gazes towards the Temple of Olympian Zeus's remains, which was under construction for 650 years: traditions are traditions.

Monument to Lord Byron.
A little further along, at the junction of Queen Amalia Avenue and Queen Olga Avenue, is another, much more noticeable and elegant monument to Lord Byron, which we are already familiar with after walking along the street named in his honor. The patron of this pompous marble composition was the prominent Greek Stefanovik Skilidis, who was also the head of the patriotic society , and in allocating funds for the monument's creation to Lord Byron in 1888, banker and entrepreneur, native of the island of Chios, Dimitrios he timed this decision to coincide with the centenary of the poet's birth. At the same time, at his suggestion, before the IV Panhellenic Olympic Games (the prototype of the future Olympic Games, held in Greece in 1859, 1870, 1875, and 1888-1889), a competition was held for prototypes of the future monument to select the best sculptor, who would be entrusted with immortalizing Byron in marble. But Skilidis was dissatisfied with the results of that competition: the author of the best prototype, the Greek Lazaros Sohos, received a prize for 2000 drachmas but, for some reason, was not invited to bring his project to life, and eventually, the creation of the monument was entrusted to the French sculptor Henri Michel Antoine Chapu. He was supposed to start work in 1891: his prototype fully satisfied Skilidis, but, as if in jest, Chapu died without ever touching the marble. After that, the creation of the sculpture, according to his project, was entrusted to another Frenchman, Jean Alexandre Joseph Falguière, who took four years to complete the order. Dimitrios Skilidis did not live to see the monument's installation: he died in 1893, and at the

solemn opening of the memorial on February 19, 1896, he was repre-
sented by the Minister of the Interior. The composition itself was magnificent: an allegory of Hellas – a semi-naked woman in a kind of chiton,
slightly larger than the figure of Byron and seemingly announcing the
poet – crowns his forehead with a palm branch. In contrast, the poet
looks at her as a child leaving his native home, with a frozen nostalgic
sadness in the gaze of a maturing youth returning to his mother. Behind

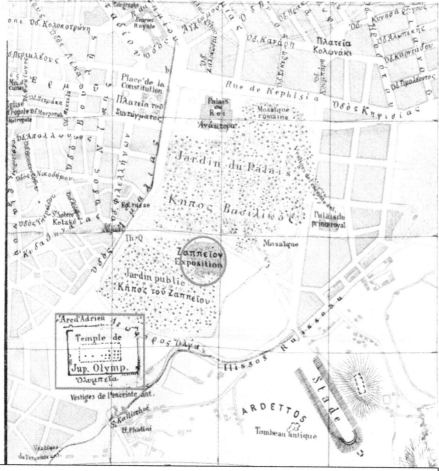

*Temple of Olympian Zeus and Hadrian's Arch (in the rectan-
gle) and the Zappion Exhibition Hall (in the circle). The 1890
map quite accurately reflects the modern geography of the
area in which we find ourselves.*

these two figures is a symbolic representation of Hellenism – a naked man, still suffering under the yoke of Ottoman rule but already ready to straighten up to full height and rise with all his pride. The inscription on the pedestal is laconic: "Hellada (Greece) – Byron." Strangely enough, after the opening, which took place shortly before the Olympic Games, many Greeks were dissatisfied with the sculpture. The newspaper "Keri" ("Times") even slammed Falguière's work: "Instead of Byron, who resembled Apollo, we see some child with disproportionate growth and an unnatural neck, while Hellada, with her hopelessly sagging, pitiful breasts, has been wrapped in some vulgar blanket. And the naked Hellen behind them, completing this ensemble, looks more like an African with his shamelessly naked body."

Roman Baths.

Continuing further along Queen Amalia Avenue, we encounter the reason why significant adjustments had to be made to the ventilation plan for the blue line of the Athens metro – the Roman public baths of the 3rd century AD, built here a few years after the destructive invasion by our friends the Goths in 267 AD. These baths were in the new Roman districts of Athens, known collectively as Hadrianoupolis, in honor of Emperor Hadrian. By the end of the 4th to the beginning of the 5th century, these baths were slightly rebuilt, expanded, and operated for quite some time. Their central and main part was a covered area where pools were located, heated from below

Ruins of Roman baths.

135

by charcoal furnaces. Baths ("Thermae") of this type were known in Greece even before its conquest by Rome and existed in large houses (mostly aristocratic) and "gymnasiums" – educational institutions. Adopted later by the Romans, the "thermae" became widespread throughout the Roman Empire, at the height of its glory stretching from the Iberian Peninsula to the territory of modern Romania and from North Africa to Scotland. Adopted by the Turks after the beginning of their close contact with Byzantium (or rather, the entire conquest of Byzantium by the Ottomans), the "thermae" were transformed into the much more familiar "hamams" in Europe today. Among the ruins, you can see a room with what seems to be remnants of columns: this is the "caldarium" – a room with hot water, and on these supports once lay a floor under which hot air heated by charcoal furnaces circulated. In front of the caldarium were two more rooms: the "tepidarium" – the "warm room," the air in which was not heated above 40°C-45°C (104°F-113°F) and used to be the central place of the baths, and the "frigidarium" – the cooling room. Now let's continue walking and, opposite the neo-Gothic Anglican Church of St. Paul, turn right onto the wonderful, wide, shady avenue. The Church of St. Paul, by the way, was built here between 1838 and 1843 from marble from Mount Hymettus and porolith from the Corinthian Isthmus, with financial support from the British government, and was supervised by Hans Christian Hansen – the elder brother of our friend Theophilus.

Monument to Ioannis Varvakis.

Monument to Ioannis Varvakis.

On this avenue, another majestic monument immortalizes the image of Ioannis Varvakis – a pirate, millionaire, nobleman, philanthropist, and... no, he probably wasn't a playboy. Varvakis did not bear this surname from birth like the previous two Ioannises we know (Macriannis and Paparrigopoulos). His father was named Andreas Leontidis (Leontis), and the word "varvakiá" is what the inhabitants of the island of Psara (Varvakis's native island) call the falcons of the species Falco eleonorae living in their lands. This same word was used in Varvakis's youth to nickname Ioannis Leontidis for his large and stern black eyes and "fiery temperament." At the beginning of his career as a pirate, he adopted "Varvakis" as his official surname. Like many other Greek pirates, he most often attacked Turkish, Egyptian, and French ships in the Aegean Sea. For the latter purpose, Greek privateers were often hired by British and Dutch fleets, wishing to prevent revolutionary France's rise as a naval power in the eastern Mediterranean. With the start of the Russo-Turkish War of 1768-1774, in which many Greeks saw a chance for their people to gain long-awaited independence, Varvakis sold most of his property to properly equip his "chebec" type ship and join the Russian Imperial Fleet in its actions off the coast of the Peloponnese. It was from his acquaintance with Russian admirals Orlov and Spiridonov and participation in the Battle of Chesma between the Russian and Turkish fleets, which ended in a decisive victory for the Russo-Greek squadron, that a new page in the life of Ioannis Varvakis could have begun, as he,

A fellow countryman of Ioannis Varvakis (also a native of the island of Psara) was another famous Greek pirate and politician - Admiral Konstantinos Canaris (not a relative of the German admiral Wilhelm Canaris). Canaris became famous for his exploits during the national liberation war of 1821-1829, especially for the destruction of several Turkish admiral ships. Canaris subsequently became Prime Minister of the Kingdom of Greece six times.

by a special decree of Empress Catherine II, was promoted to the rank of lieutenant in the Russian Imperial Fleet. However, after the war, Varvakis returned to piracy, and what ultimately led him to end his career under sail was an incident in Constantinople when his ship was confiscated during an attempt to sell it, despite the Greek pirate's arrival in the capital of the Ottoman Empire without any fear of arrest. Naturally fearing arrest and execution, Varvakis managed to escape from Constantinople to Odessa and from there to St. Petersburg, where he received a warm reception from Catherine II, who put him in charge of extracting and preparing black caviar in the Caspian Sea. So Varvakis became the first exporter of caviar to Europe. In 1789, he was granted Russian citizenship and ennobled. By then, enterprising Ioannis Varvakis had already amassed a considerable fortune from the caviar trade and acquired his small trading fleet. Nearly thirty years later, in 1821, the 76-year-old Varvakis entered into close relations with the organizers of the Greek underground patriotic organization "Filiki Eteria" – Count Ioannis Kapodistrias and Alexandros Ypsilantis: until 1824, he supplied Greek rebels with weapons, purchasing them in his name at Imperial factories in Russia and, through the Constantinople Patriarchate, ransoming compatriots captured by the Turks. But after the massacre by the Turks on Varvakis's native island of Psara, resulting in the deaths of about 20,000 Greeks, the former pirate, now a 78-year-old man, armed a ship and sailed to Greece himself, where he was destined to face God. Early in the morning on January 12, 1825, Ioannis Varvakis died in a British hospital on the island of Zakynthos from the effects of a severe infectious disease. In his will, Varvakis instructed using 1,000,000 Russian rubles from his funds to establish an academy in future-free Greece, sell most of his movable and immovable property, and donate the proceeds to the Greek government for other charitable purposes. That very million remained in a Russian bank account until 1857, when, under the guidance of Panagis Kalkos, the construction of the "Varvakis School" began, which operated as a practical high school of natural sciences from 1886. Another part of the funds he donated was used to open the central covered market of Athens in 1886 – the "Varvakeios Agora." This monument to Ioannis Varvakis was commissioned by the Greek government from Professor Leonidas Drosis and installed here in 1889, with the official unveiling taking place a year later, coinciding with the solemn reburial of Varvakis at the First Athens Cemetery. At the base, where the figure of the glorious Greek pirate-philanthropist stands, the sculptor depicted four allegorical figures: Free Greece, Thought, Navigation, and History – the four main companions of Varvakis's life.

The Zappeion Exhibition Hall.

The Zappeion Exhibition Hall.

A shady alley leads us to the large building of the Zappeion Exhibition Hall – another architectural masterpiece by Theophilus von Hansen, built by the order and with full funding from Evangelos and Constantinos Zappas – two more great national benefactors of the Greek people, whose surname is associated with the history of the revival of the Olympic Games. Held for 1170 years every 4 years (from 776 BC to 394 AD), the ancient Olympic Games were among the many ancient Greek celebrations dedicated to all the Gods of Olympus. The classical competitions of the ancient Olympiads were the Pentathlon (running, long jump with weights in hands, javelin throw, discus throw, and wrestling) and chariot races. Like many other sports competitions and mysteries held in honor of various pagan Gods of the ancient Greek pantheon, they were banned in the late 4th century by the Roman Emperor Theodosius I, who launched a comprehensive Christianization of the Empire. From

Constantinos Zappas
(1814-1892).

that time until the mid-19th century, no comparable sporting events to the ancient Olympics in scale were held. It was only in 1856 that a wealthy Greek entrepreneur from Wallachia (the territory of modern Romania), Evangelos Zappas, approached King Otto I of Greece with a proposal to revive the Olympic movement, primarily as a means of "resurrecting," or rather, creating a new Greek national consciousness. Zappas was willing to finance the entire project himself and also proposed to involve representatives of other nations in the Olympic Games, thus initiating the establishment of something akin to the International Olympic Committee. Alexandros Rizos Rangavis, the Minister of Foreign Affairs of the Greek Kingdom, was skeptical of Zappas's proposal, saying that "today nations do not excel in good athletes, but rather in pioneers of industry and agriculture" and suggested that the entrepreneur finance a large industrial exhibition in Athens. However, Zappas persisted, and after lengthy negotiations with His Majesty and after a series of publications defending the

Ticket to the first Greek Olympic Games in 1859.

idea of reviving the Olympic Games in the Greek newspapers, which formed a certain group of advocates for this initiative, a royal decree was signed to organize the first sports competitions of this kind at the national level. They took place in 1859, in Ludovic Square (now known as Omonia Square) and were attended by representatives of various professions and social strata: farmers, gendarmes, and even a blind beggar who "miraculously regained his sight and competed in the race." The disciplines in which the first Greek Olympians competed after almost 1500 years were classical: only wrestling was absent, and equestrian competitions replaced the chariot race. Evangelos Zappas was pleased with the lively interest in sports competitions aroused in society and was determined to finance similar Olympic Games permanently. Still, he died suddenly in 1865, before age 65, leaving behind a colossal fortune, which was bequeathed to the cause of promoting and developing sports games in Greece and worldwide. Evangelos Zappas appointed his cousin, Constantinos Zappas, responsible for fulfilling his last will. The latter turned to the government of the Greek Kingdom with a proposal to build a large exhibition hall where an "Olympic exhibition" of achievements in industry and agriculture could be held every four years. In 1869, a plot of land measuring 80,000 square meters (861,112 square feet) between the Royal Palace and the ruins of the Temple of Olympian Zeus was allocated for the construction of this building. After a series of delays associated with the development of the building project and the replacement of the Frenchman Francois Boulanger by Theophilus von Hansen as the chief architect, the exhibition hall was laid in 1874. It was ceremonially opened on October 20, 1888. By then, the first public sports complex in Greece had already been built with the funds of the late Evangelos Zappas – the Gymnasium, opposite the Panathenaic Stadium (Kallimarmaro) on the present-day King Constantine I Avenue. In the same year, 1888, the last IV National Olympiad of Greece took

Evangelos Zappas (1800-1865).

place, after which Crown Prince of Greece Constantine proposed to organize Olympic competitions every 4 years on a permanent basis. Based on this, the following games were supposed to take place in 1892, but they were never held due to lack of funds. After the death of Constan-

View of the monument to Evangelos Zappas through the colonnade and façade of the Zappion exhibition hall.

tinos Zappas, monuments to both patrons of sports were installed at the entrance to the exhibition hall, named after them – the Zappeion. In 1896, during the I International Olympic Games, fencing competitions were held in this building, where the Greeks managed to win five medals: two gold (rapier among maestros and sabre), one silver (sabre), and two bronze (rapiers). During the extraordinary Olympic Games of 1906, also held in Athens, the Zappeion played the role of the "Olympic Village," during the 2004 Olympic Games, it housed an information center. Also, in the ceremonial hall of the Zappeion, there is a crypt where the head of Evangelos Zappas was placed: it is embedded in the wall and sealed with a beautiful marble plaque.

Sculpture "Lumberjack".

Now let's move further, past the "Zappeion," along the dirt alley that leads us through the park to the very stadium where the first international Olympic Games of 1896 took place – the "Panathenaic Stadium"

The sculpture is in its old place, on Queen Amalia Avenue.

("Panafinaiki Stadium"), also called by the Athenians "Kallimarmaro" – "Beautiful Marble." Before it appears before us, however, we will notice at the exit of the alley a marble sculpture of a naked man facing us with an unexpected side. That's the "Lumberjack" by the Greek sculptor Dimitris Philippotis (1839-1919). It was commissioned by the Mayor of Athens, Spiridon Mercouris, the grandfather of the already famous Melina Mercouri, to adorn Queen Amalia Avenue near the Byzantine church of the Holy Trinity in 1908. However, in 1910 and 1912, the sculpture was heavily damaged by unknown vandals: the first one splashed red paint mixed with some corrosive chemicals onto the face of the marble lumberjack, while the second one mutilated the sculpture in the genital area. After restoration, the sculpture was returned to its place, but in 1960, it was decided to install it here, opposite the stadium.

Panathenaic Stadium ("Kallimarmaro").

View from the top of Kalimarmaro Stadium, 2024.

The public watches the opening ceremony of the first Olympic Games, 1896.

HRH Crown Prince Constantine, future King of the Hellines (Greeks) Constantine I.

However, let's not waste any more time approaching it. I won't argue that "Kallimarmaro" is impressive: 50 rows of marble benches can accommodate about 80,000 spectators. The uniqueness of the stadium is that it was entirely built exclusively from Pentelic marble – the same marble from which the ancient Parthenon was built, with the only difference being that the stadium acquired its present form only on the eve of 1896. Of course, it was not built on an empty site: the ancient "Panathenaic Stadium" was erected here, between Ardittos Hill and the Ilissos River (now beneath you, in the sewer), already in the 4th century BCE for hosting the Panathenaic Games (athletic competitions dedicated to the goddess Athena, held only in this city). The first competitions were held here in 330-329

Monument to Georgios Averoff in front of Kalimarmaro Stadium.

BCE, and during the time of Herodes Atticus (139-144 CE), the stadium was significantly expanded, acquiring a horseshoe shape and since then accommodating up to 50,000 spectators. Then, a sanctuary of the ancient Greek Goddess of Luck – Tyche – adorned with ivory and gold, appeared on the top of Ardittos Hill. Several stones from the sanctuary's foundation can still be seen at the top if you want to climb up there. The stadium's fate is not known for certain, but at some point, it was almost completely dismantled after the advent of Christianity in Athens. Apparently, after the prohibition of sports competitions as pagan rituals contrary to the new Christian dogma, the marble was used to construct Christian churches and residential buildings. In the 13th and 14th centuries, the Frankish dukes ruling in Athens turned the stadium into an arena for conducting knightly tournaments. Still, by the beginning of the

19th century, only a few remnants of its foundation and the "Cave of Destiny" remained – the only untouched part of the modern stadium since ancient times. This cave, 57 meters long and about 4 meters wide (177 by 13 feet), existed in Ardittos Hill even before it was decided to build a sports facility here. According to a widespread legend, it was inhabited by the Moirai – the ancient Greek Goddesses of fate, spinning "the threads of our lives." In Roman times, when the ancient stadium was used as a Colosseum, the animals and people participating in the battles there entered the arena through this cave, which was turned into a tunnel. In this tunnel, from the moment Greece gained independence from the Ottoman Empire until 1850, a slaughterhouse was located; today, this cave is part of the gallery leading to the stadium's interior, where there is a small Olympic museum and a souvenir shop. Evangelos Zappas turned his attention to the remnants of the ancient stadium in 1856: at that time, he was ready to finance its restoration and the construction of an exhibition hall, later known as the "Zappeion." However, during Evangelos's lifetime, these projects were not implemented: the stadium's reconstruction began only in 1874 with the funds he bequeathed. Then, a bridge was built over the still-flowing river Ilissos in front of the stadium (part of which is now in the sewers), and the stadium largely acquired its modern features. However, in preparation for the first Olympics in 1896, it was decided to expand and improve the stadium. Crown Prince Constantine, who took responsibility for the preparatory work as head of the Olympic Games Commission (the future International Olympic Committee), turned to another great Greek benefactor (yes, there were many in the 19th century), Georgios Averof, for funding the project. After the death of Evangelos Zappas in 1865, Averof, possibly the wealthiest subject of the Greek King, was ready to finance all the required work fully. Moreover, he allocated a sum several times larger than that initially requested by Prince Constantine: 1,000,000 drachmas. With this money, the project by Ernst Ziller and Greek architect Anastasios Metaxas to transform the Panathenaic Stadium into the main venue for the Olympic Games was implemented. Despite not completing the work by 1896, the 1896 Olympics were held with great pomp. Since then, this stadium has been an essential "participant" in most Olympic ceremonies and other sporting events, hosting exhibitions and concerts and serving as a museum at different times.

Monument to Georgios Karaiskakis.

Following from the stadium towards the National Garden (crossing King

Constantine I Avenue again) along Herod Atticus Street, you will see on a small square to your left the equestrian monument to Georgios Karaiskakis – one of the many leaders of the Greek War of Independence of 1821-1829, under whose command the Greek rebels attempted to lift the Turkish siege of the Acropolis in 1827 (we discussed these events when recalling Sir Richard Church). If you remember how many years the Athens municipality and the Greek Ministry of Culture deliberated on where to place the monument to Alexander the Great, then prepare to be horrified: the same authorities could not decide on a location for Karaiskakis' equestrian statue for almost 40 years (from 1929 to 1968). The author of this monument – Greek sculptor Michalis Tombros – led the Athens School of Fine Arts from 1957 to 1959, and his student was Spyros (Spyridon) Gogos – the author of the monument to the final Emperor of Byzantium, Constantine XI, which we are already familiar with. Comparing that sculpture with the monument to Karaiskakis, I believe the student surpassed his teacher. However, I could be mistaken.

The New Royal Palace (the residence of the President of Greece).
Adjacent to Herodu Attikou Street is the fence of the Royal Garden, now known as the National Garden. Soon, we will take a short walk through it, but let's look closely at the other side, where the New Royal Palace

The New Royal Palace.

(now called the Presidential Palace) is located. This luxurious residence was built according to the design... yes, you probably remembered two names, and one of them, of course, hit the mark – Ernst Ziller, who was appointed court architect by His Majesty the King of the Greeks, George I, and designed, in total, about 700 buildings throughout Greece. The king issued the decree allocating funds for the construction of the palace and the preparation of projects in the year of the birth of his firstborn and heir to the throne – Prince Constantine – in 1868. The work began in 1891 and was completed six years later. It is also worth noting that Theophilus Hansen indirectly contributed to this palace. In preparing his drawings, Ziller used Hansen's unrealized project to construct a summer palace for the Royal Family. Immediately after the

King Constantine and Queen Consort Sophia (sister of the German Kaiser Wilhelm) in their study in the New Royal Palace. February 1921.

completion of the construction, Crown Prince Constantine moved into this residence with his wife, Princess Sophia (sister of the German Emperor Wilhelm II), and their young children: Prince George (future King George II), Prince Alexander (future King Alexander I), and Princess Helen (future Queen Consort of Romania). After 1909, the entire Greek royal family lived in this palace for a long time. On the eve of Christmas 1909, the Old Royal Palace on Constitution Square was almost destroyed by fire. Until 1913, this palace was called the Palace of the Crown Prince. Still, after King George I was shot by a Greek anarchist while walking along the promenade in Thessaloniki in 1913 (after 50 years of reign), his son did not move to the Old Royal Palace on Constitution Square. Then, the Royal Court moved here, and the widowed Queen Olga continued to live in the old palace. At the request of Constantine I, Ziller added a large ballroom to this palace, where state award ceremonies were also held. Since then, the New Royal Palace has changed owners quite often. After the abdication of King Constantine I during the state coup in 1917, his younger son – elevated to the throne by Venizelos as Alexander I – lived in the palace. After the sudden death of the latter in 1920, the palace was again occupied by the returning Constantine I from exile, but in 1922, he was again forced to abdicate the throne, this time in favor of his elder son, George II. He was also overthrown in the 1924 revolution, after which the New Royal Palace was declared the residence of the president of the Second Hellenic Republic. In the 11 years of its existence, three presidents succeeded each other, after which, in 1935, the monarchy was restored in the country, and King George II again occupied the palace. He left it next time only in 1941: shortly before German troops occupied Athens, the King and his entire government were evacuated to the island of Crete and from there –to Alexandria. Later, George II said that "the most necessary thing for a Greek monarch is a suitcase." He returned to Athens in September 1946, and after his childless death on April 1, 1947, the new owner of this palace became his younger brother – King Paul I. The last crowned inhabitant of this residence was the son of Paul I – King Constantine II, who was forced to flee from Greece after the military coup in December 1967. The president has occupied this palace since the fall of the "Black Colonels" military junta in 1974 and the proclamation of the Third Hellenic Republic. Formally, the president is the head of state; however, Greece, like most former monarchies of Europe, is a parliamentary republic in which the head of the government and prime minister are the de facto head of state. You can take a photo with the evzones standing at the palace gates. Still, only with the permission of the responsible officer: usually, he stands nearby, in field uniform and a beret.

Maximos Mansion (residence of the Prime Minister of Greece).

Interestingly, just across the road from the New Royal Palace is the "Megaron Maximou" – the "Maximos Mansion" – the equivalent of

London's residence at 10 Downing Street. Construction of this mansion began only in 1912; there was an empty lot here before that. And no, to anticipate your assumptions, I hasten to disappoint you: neither

Ernst Ziller nor Theophilus Hansen had anything to do with this mansion's construction or architectural plans. The master who worked on it was a Greek, Anastasios Helmis (you may not remember this name, unlike Ziller and Hansen; it will not come up again). The client was... yes, you guessed it: the wealthy Greek shipowner Alexandros Michalinos. Unfortunately, he did not live to see the completion of the construction, and after he died in 1916, his widow Irini remarried. Her new husband was the banker and economist Dimitrios Maximos, after whom this mansion would be named. From 1916 to 1921, the unfinished residence was owned by Leonidas Embirikos, who completed the construction and then sold it back to the Maximos couple. They lived there until 1952, when the Greek government approached Dimitrios Maximos with an offer to purchase the mansion for 11 billion drachmas (a very substantial sum at that time). However, Maximos, a patriot at heart (though more likely driven by a desire to enter the country's history), announced his willingness to give his house to the government for half the offered amount, and even with all the furniture and the collection of paintings and sculptures in it, with just one condition: this mansion

The first owner of the building was Dimitrios Maximos (1873-1955). By the way, he also managed to be Prime Minister of Greece from January 24 to August 29, 1947.

should be used as an "official residence" and for hosting foreign heads of state. That's how the "Megaron Maximou" became Greece's property. Since then, and until 1982, heads of state visiting Athens with official visits stayed in this house (for example, in 1980, the Prime Minister of the United Kingdom, Margaret Thatcher, stayed here). An interesting incident occurred in 1967. At that time, the family of Lieutenant General Georgios Zoitakis – the former aide-de-camp to King Paul I of Greece, appointed regent of the Greek Kingdom after the expulsion of King Constantine II by the "Black Colonels" coup – moved into the "Megaron Maximou." Like most junta members, Zoitakis came from a peasant background, and his wife, Sofia, although a graduate of the Faculty of Philosophy, was quite practical. When she became the "mistress" of the Maximos mansion, she often lamented that "there is no point in these palaces: you can't even set up a chicken coop here." Arguing with her was, of course, difficult.

Royal (National) Garden.
You can enter the former Royal and now National Garden from Herodou Attikou Street through three entrances, but since the garden itself is not very large, you won't get lost anyway. It should be noted that there are quite a few interesting sights: monuments to Greek political and cultural figures, Roman ruins, beautiful alleys, and a living corner with goats, geese, rabbits, ducks, and turtles. In the summer, you may also come across Balkan turtles crawling along the paths—a subspecies of the Mediterranean turtle, whose shell reaches 30, sometimes 40

centimeters in length, and their average lifespan is about 90 years. The two most prominent monuments in the garden are the busts of the first president of Greece, Count Ioannis Kapodistrias, and the "friend of the Greeks," the patron, and one of the pioneers of the daguerreotype, Jean-Gabriel Eynard. The latter entered Greek history because, since 1825, he was one of the main sponsors of the Greek rebels. After the War of Independence ended, he donated 700,000 francs for the country's reconstruction (or rather, construction). In 1847, he also contributed to the repayment of the external debt of the Greek Kingdom for a loan from fifteen years ago, paying half a million francs to the Greek government. These two busts are located in the southern part of the park, near the Roman ruins, at the exit to the Zappeion Ex-

Count Dionysios Solomos (1798-1857) – author of the poem, part of which is known today as the Greek anthem.

hibition Hall. In the eastern part, there is a bust of Dionysios Solomos – one of the great modern Greek poets, the author of the words of the Greek anthem – "Hymn to Liberty." There is a common misconception that the Greek anthem is the longest national anthem in the world, supposedly consisting of 158 verses. The entire poem by Dionysios Solomos, written in 1823, consists of 158 verses, of which only the first 24 were declared the national anthem of the Kingdom of Greece in 1865. In practice, in the overwhelming many cases, only the first two verses are performed:

I know you from the blade.
Of the sword, the terrifying [blade],
I know you from your appearance,
Which, with force, measures the earth.

From the bones taken out,
the sacred (bones) of Greeks
And as first brave again,
Rejoice, oh rejoice, liberty!

The initiator of the entire garden was Queen Consort of Greece, Amalia, the spouse of King Otto I. Her grandfather, the Grand Duke of Oldenburg (since 1918, the Grand Duchy of Oldenburg has been part of Ger-

Monuments to Jean-Gabriel Einard and Count Kapodistrias in the Royal Garden.

many), Peter Friedrich Ludwig, had a great passion for gardening and created a luxurious palace garden at his residence in Oldenburg, which was one of the first publicly accessible palace gardens in Europe. This family tradition played its role when Amalia became the Greek Queen through marriage to Otto. She began working on the arrangement of

Roman ruins and a two-hundred-year-old cypress tree in the Royal Garden.

her future palace garden even before the completion of the Royal Palace – in 1838 by inviting the German agronomist Friedrich Schmidt, who brought more than 500 species of plants for the garden. Unfortunately, most of them did not survive: the dry Mediterranean climate proved lethal for them. After Schmidt, botanists Karl Nicolaus Fraas, Theodor von Heldreich, and the Greek Spiridon Miliaritis worked on the garden. Among the trees planted in the garden were North American Washingtonia palms (the first of which, at the central entrance to the garden, was planted by Queen Amalia herself), almonds, plane trees, cypresses, and South American agaves. The latter appealed so much to Amalia's courtiers that soon, agaves appeared in the suburban gardens of all affluent Athenians, and from there, they spread almost throughout Greece. Pay attention to the thickets of these plants during your upcoming ascent to Lycabettus.

The Benaki Museum.

After strolling enough in the Royal (National) Garden, head to Queen Sophia Avenue. On the opposite side of the garden, at the intersection with Kymbari Street, which continues the Herod Atticus Street, there is a neoclassical mansion of the Benaki family, where the stunning collection of the Benaki Museum is housed. The museum's founder, Antonis

Benakis, a member of one of Greece's wealthiest dynasties, began assembling his collection of ancient, medieval, Byzantine, and Islamic art objects in the late 19th century, traveling to Egypt. After 30 years of continuous expansion of his collection 1926, he donated all his home museum exhibits to the Greek government, along with his father's mansion – Emmanuel Benakis. Now, in the 36 halls of this building, a large part of the Benaki collection is presented, with exhibits arranged in chronological order: from archaeological finds from the Paleolithic era to the period of the Greek War of Independence and the mid-19th century. There are also several branches of the Benaki Museum, one of which – in the Kerameikos area – exhibits Islamic art objects covering the period from the 7th to the early 20th century.

Palace of the Officers' Club. (Rigillis 1, Athina 106 75)

Further along Queen Sophia Avenue, we will come across the Palace of the Officers' Club of the Greek Armed Forces, known as "Sarogleio Megaron" – named after General Petros Saroglou, who allocated a substantial sum from his will to construct the club. Nowadays, this magnificent Baroque-style building hosts solemn dinners for officers and their families, as well as houses a museum with limited access and a barbershop for club members.

Palace of the Officers' Club.

Estate of the Duchess of Piacenza (Byzantine Museum).

Adjacent to this building is the extensive garden of the Duchess of Piacenza's estate, where the superb

Byzantine Christian Museum is located today. This luxurious estate in the Byzantine style was built by order of Sophie de Marbois-Lebrun (born Barbé-Marbois), who held the title of Duchess of Piacenza by marriage. The life story of this extravagant lady, born in Pennsylvania to a French American family, could have been made into a Quentin Tarantino film: the material for the screenplay in the best traditions of this

Gate of the estate of the Duchess of Piacenza (Byzantine Museum).

director is astonishing. At the age of 17, Sophie Barbé-Marbois, the daughter of the French consul general to the United States and the granddaughter of the governor of Pennsylvania (on her mother's side) married Anne-Charles Lebrun, the son of the chief treasurer of the French Empire and one of the three (alongside Napoleon Bonaparte) former consuls of the Republic Charles-François Lebrun. It was he, Charles-François, who, for his work in annexing the Italian region of Liguria, was granted the title of Duke of Piacenza by Napoleon I (before that, the duchy belonged to one of the bourbon lines). After Charles-François died in 1809, his son, Anne-Charles, became the new Duke of Piacenza, and Sophie, consequently, the Duchess. However, Sophie and Lebrun's marriage did not last: almost immediately after the birth of their only daughter, Élisa, in 1804, the spouses effectively separated but continued to maintain friendly relations through correspondence, and the divorce was officially finalized only in 1831. In Paris, the Duchess lived a lavish lifestyle, establishing a luxurious literary salon and becoming one of the centers of attraction for the entire high society of the city. For example, in 1826, Sophie Lebrun met Count Ioannis Kapodistrias – a former Minister of Foreign Affairs of the Russian Empire and the future first President of Greece. Kapodistrias impressed the Duchess with his erudition, refinement, and nobility, and after the count left Paris, they began corresponding. Their next meeting in Rome in 1827, when Kapodistrias had already been elected temporary ruler of Greece and was preparing to depart for the Peloponnese,

Sophie de Marbois, duchess of Piacenza (1785-1854).

radically changed Sophie's life. "The ancient homeland of arts, sciences, and philosophy, the native land of Socrates, Plato, Pericles, and Homer, is fighting for its independence from the 'foreign yoke' that has tormented the Hellenic people for four centuries" – agree, it sounds romantic. From the moment of this second meeting between the Duchess of Piacenza and Kapodistrias, the woman became an active member of the French Philhellenic Committee and, after selling her jewelry for 14,000 francs, adding another 9,000 to this amount, she donated this money to the temporary government of Greece for the organization of primary education in the future state. Soon, her daughter Élisa joined her mother's endeavors. Almost immediately after the end of hostilities, in December 1829, the Duchess of Piacenza and her daughter arrived in Nafplion – the first capital of Greece, a port town, and a former colony of Venice on the Peloponnese peninsula. There, Kapodistrias formed his first government, and Sophie Lebrun became involved in the political life of the young republic. However, she soon became disillusioned with her old friend: in his attempts to bring order to the young country, where almost every armed man saw himself as a ruler (presi-

Main house of the estate.

dent, king, or even emperor), Count Kapodistrias resorted to harsh methods, and many yesterday's war heroes found themselves in prisons and exile. In these actions, Sophie Lebrun saw excessive despotism and opposed the count and just a year after living in Nafplion, she left for the island of Aegina and from there – to Italy, where she learned about the murder of Kapodistrias. According to some historians, the Duchess of Piacenza advocated for the murderer – Konstantinos Mavromichalis, who was lynched by a crowd at the scene of the crime. In one way or another, in 1833, Sophie and Élisa returned to Greece. They settled in its new capital, Athens, where the duchess bought extensive land in empty fields far beyond the city, connecting Athens to the port of Piraeus. There, she settled in a two-story wooden house, which took two years to build. During all this time, Sophie and her

Not only the French became philhellenes, but the Greeks also became great «philofrancs». Few people know, but during the famous Egyptian campaign of Napoleon Bonaparte, 1,500 Greek volunteers served in his army, forming their Greek Legion under the command of a former military man in the service of the Ottoman Sultan Nikolaos Papazoglou. After the end of the Egyptian campaign, the remnants of the Greek Legion followed Bonaparte to France and remained loyal to him until his exile to the island of St. Helena.

daughter Élisa lived in the "Europe" hotel – the first hotel in Athens, and most likely, the Duchess of Piacenza was excessively protective of her daughter, as by that time Élisa was already 31 years old. Still, no news of her supposed engagements with anyone has reached us. It is quite possible that Sophie Lebrun was afraid of loneliness because, apart from her daughter, there was no one else in her life. Therefore, she prevented any opportunities for Élisa to marry. The following fact confirms Sophie's theory of "hyper-guardianship" over her daughter. In 1835, the Duchess and her daughter embarked on a journey through Ottoman Syria and Lebanon, during which Élisa contracted the plague and died in her mother's arms. The grief that befell Sophie Lebrun was so heavy that she ordered her daughter's body to be embalmed, paid for its transportation to Athens, and exhibited it in an open coffin in the basement of her house, where she arranged something like a chapel. In addition, she decided to buy land on Mount Pendeli to build a magnificent temple in memory of Élisa and bury her there. Still, this idea was vehemently opposed by the monks of the Orthodox monastery on Pendeli, which had been active since the 16th century. Prime Minister of Greece, the Francophile Ioannis Kolettis, had to intervene in the matter, and he managed to persuade the monks to sell part of the land on the mountain top in exchange for financing the construction of a bridge, road construction, and the development of two marble quarries by the Duchess. Thus, in 1840, she became the owner of 1738 acres of land in the area of Mount Pendeli, where, according to the project of Stamatis Cleanthes and under the guidance of Hans Christian Hansen, four houses were started to be built: "Castello Rododafni" – the main residence of the Duchess, from which she planned to observe the construction of the mausoleum-temple of her daughter; "Plaisance" – named after her title (in French, the city of Piacenza is called Plaisance); "Maisonette" and "Tourelle" ("Tower"). At the same time, Cleanthes began the construction of this very villa – "Ilissia," on the land purchased by the Duchess in the scorched steppes at a sufficient distance from Athens (yes, today it is almost the center of the city, but at that time there was nothing around the Duchess's house except fields and boulders). The construction of this estate took seven years, and a year before its completion, the Duchess of Piacenza suffered a new blow, after which her mental state was shaken. Sophie Lebrun's "temporary" wooden house, located on the Piraeus road, burned to the ground on the night of December 19, 1847, and along with it, the embalmed body of her daughter, Élisa, burned down. The woman was completely inconsolable, and after that, she stopped appearing at the Royal Court and ceased to respond to letters. She ended her relationship quite coldly with Stamatis Cleanthes and Christian Hansen after finishing her new home "Ilissia." She lived the remaining six years in this estate almost like a recluse, indulging in various eccentricities. Thus, Sophie Lebrun officially renounced Catholicism and underwent the rite of Orthodox baptism. Still, shortly after that, she renounced Orthodoxy and converted to Judaism, after which she financed the construction of a synagogue in the city of Chalkida on the island of Euboea. In her house, she gathered the most diverse guests, from foreign travelers to gypsy fortune tellers, and formed something like her own "court," granting noble titles to her friends. Additionally, the Duchess practically fully supported the family of the Consul General of Portugal, a Jew by origin, David Bonifacio Pacifico, who lived in her house, with whom one long and unsightly story is connected, which led to a diplomatic scandal between Greece and Great Britain. Also, shortly before her move to the villa "Ilisia," the Duchess of Piacenza was abducted by a gang of Greek bandits led by Spiros Bibisis, who operated on the highways near Athens in the first decades after Greece gained independence. The bandits captured her during a trip to the construction site of her daughter's funerary temple in Pendeli. She was held by Bibisis and his men for several days, during which the criminals demanded a ransom from the Greek government for the duchess. The story ended with the lady's rescue from the hands of the bandits by enraged residents of Chalandri – a suburb of Athens whom Sophie Lebrun had befriended. The paradox of this story was that after her release, the duchess actively advocated for her kidnapper and pleaded for his pardon, giving rise to rumors of their secret love affair and staging the abduction. In her final years, Sophie Lebrun, the Duchess of Piacenza, almost ceased to receive visitors and only communicated with Photini Mavromihalis – the lady-in-waiting of Queen Amalia and the niece of the murderer of Count Capodistrias, Konstantinos Mavromihalis. Most of her architectural whims near Pendeli, built under the direction of Hans Christian Hansen, were completed after the duchess died in 1854, and the villa "Ilisia," where we are now, was handed over to the Greek Ministry of Defense, which owned it until 1930 when it became the Byzantine Museum. It houses a rich collection of icons, church utensils, coins, Roman and

Hans Christian Hansen (1803-1883). Elder brother of Theophilus von Hansen, hired by the Duchess to carry out her ambitious projects.

Byzantine sculptures, and a copy of the famous mosaic from the Basilica of San Vitale in Ravenna depicting Emperor Justinian I with his courtiers. Despite all her eccentricities, the Duchess of Piacenza entered Greek history as a benefactress, greatly contributing to the Greek insurgents during their struggle for independence from the Ottoman Empire and regularly making donations for various purposes after her move to Athens. Everything she promised the monks in Pendeli was fulfilled by her: the duchess's bridge still stands and bears her name, as does the metro station on the blue line, which opened on the eve of the 2004 Olympic Games.

Military History Museum.

Installation in the backyard of the Military History Museum.

Immediately behind the "Ilisia" estate is the huge Military History Museum of the Ministry of Defense, which, in addition to artifacts telling the military history of Greece from the Bronze Age (until the 13th century BCE) to the conflict in Cyprus (1974), features an impressive collection of weapons and armor belonging to General Petros Saroglou: medieval European, Japanese, Turkish, Arab weapons, and much more. And in a small garden near the main entrance, a cafe in a military truck serves delicious Greek coffee.

Kolonaki district.

Suppose you cross Queen Sophia Avenue opposite the War Museum and walk up Plutarch Street. In that case, you'll find yourself in one of the most aristocratic and prestigious neighborhoods in today's Athens – Kolonaki. This neighborhood grew at the foot of Mount Lycabettus – the highest point in the city – in the second half of the 19th century, thanks to the proximity of the Royal Palace. Since then, Kolonaki has been home to politicians, lawyers, actors, writers, artists, entrepreneurs, and bankers – the Greek nation's most illustrious and distinguished members. However, even during Ottoman rule, these areas were called "Katsikadika" from the word "katsika," meaning "goat," as Athenian shepherds grazed their dairy goats on the slopes of Lycabet-

Kolonaki, Patriarchou Joachim street, 2024.

tus from this side. Ironically, isn't it? The neighborhood's current name comes from the familiar word "column," and means "small column". It is associated with an even earlier tradition than goat grazing, of ancient Athenians offering sacrifices of small animals in the grove on the slopes of Mount Lycabettus for healing purposes. Marble columns of small dimensions were erected at the sites of such sacrifices (one of the found ones was 2 meters (6.6 feet) in height and 30 centimeters (12 inches) in

Kolonaki, Patriarchou Joachim street, 1924.

Street fighting in Athens between British troops and Greek communist strike groups in December 1944 –1945 January.

dIameter), and this tradition, it is believed, persisted even after the Christianization of Athens. Among old Athenians (mostly communists), there was another nickname for the neighbourhood – "Skobia," after British Lieutenant General Sir Ronald Scobie, who commanded the III Corps of the British Army sent to Greece to assist local partisans in expelling the Germans but then played a key role in the ensuing Greek Civil War. Britain supported the legitimate government of the Greek Kingdom (King George II and His government in exile) and sided with the monarchist partisans. At the same time, most participants in the Greek resistance to the German occupation were members of the communist underground and aimed to overthrow

One of the streets in the Kolonaki area leading to Lycabettus Hill. At the end of the street you can see the main house of the estate of the Duchess of Piacenza.

the monarchy and turn Greece into a socialist republic. Armed clashes between Greek communists and the British army supporting the royal government took place on the streets of Athens, but only for 1 month, 1 week, and 1 day (from December 3, 1944, to January 11, 1945). During these events, a British army artillery battery was stationed at the top of Lycabettus and fired on areas where communist fighters barricaded themselves. At the same time, in the Kolonaki neighbourhood itself, General Scobie set up his headquarters; thus, the nickname "Skobia" stuck to the neighbourhood. When Plutarch Street meets Patriarch Joachim Street (Ioakeim), turn onto it (left) and walk on the odd-numbered side until you see the red sign for "Mailo's" – they serve the most delicious, diverse, and inexpen sive pasta in the city. This little restaurant is one of the fast-food establishments, and you may have already noticed their signs near Constitution Square or somewhere in Pagrati. The chain expanded during the coronavirus pandemic, and I have repeatedly found no better place for a pleasant and quick meal during walks around the city when your schedule is filled with sights. When Patriarch Joachim

Typical Kolonaki cigar kiosk.

Street meets the now fenced-off and excavated Kolonaki Square (also known as "Filikis Eterias" Square) for the construction of the fourth metro line, continue until you reach the turn onto Skoufa Street and look at the assortment in the local kiosks – "periptero." Kolonaki is one of the two neighbourhoods in Athens known to me where cigars are sold at the kiosks, so you know exactly how prestigious and affluent your neighborhood is.

Orthodox Church of Saint Dionysius.

Located on Skoufa Street is the Orthodox Church of Saint Dionysius the Areopagite – one of the architectural masterpieces of Athens that many tour guides and guidebooks unjustly overlook. This massive church, combining elements of neo-Baroque and neoclassical styles, may seem quite old, but it has not even reached a hundred years. It was founded in 1925 by the design of Anastasios Orlandos and consecrated by Archbishop of Athens and All Greece Chrysostomos I in 1931. It served as the Cathedral of the Greek Orthodox Church for some time, while the well-known Virgin Mary's Cathedral of the Annunciation was closed for

168

Orthodox Church of Saint Dionysius.

restoration. Next to the thirty years with the aroma of coffee, fresh pastries, and exquisite desserts. I can't say that I visit it often. Still, suppose you want to admire the church and fully experience the cathedral is the cozy café attracted locals for atmosphere of this neighbourhood. In that case, I won't dissuade you from enjoying a cup of espresso, especially since we have a journey ahead of us – up to Lycabettus.

Lycabettus Hill.

Church of St. George on top of Lycabettus Hill.

The shortest way to it lies through Dimokritou Street (intersecting Skoufa Street right before the St. Dionysius Temple). This street ends at a staircase leading to a dead end, and if you turn right from it and climb another staircase, you'll find yourself on *Stratiotikou Syndesmou Street*. Moving along it, under the shade of spreading plane trees, turn left at the first turn and continue upwards until you reach the junction with Kleomenous Street. When you reach the last street, turn left at the first intersection with the pedestrian street Lukianu (Loukianou). Yes, this entire street consists of stairs, and after climbing one flight up, you'll find yourself at the beginning of the shortest pedestrian path to the top of Lycabettus. If you don't feel up for amateur climbing (actually, the path up isn't that scary), you can use the tunnel funicular. Its station is five minutes from you, on Aristippou Street: the cable cars run constantly up and down, and one funicular ticket costs 7 euros. If you have decided to walk up to Lycabettus, then halfway to the top, you will be greeted by a pleasant surprise in the form of a café on the terrace with a decent view. But the views from the café at the city's highest point will be much better, just a few dozen meters away (nothing at all). The first thing you will see when you climb up is the incomparable panorama of Athens, Piraeus, and the suburbs, and on a clear day, the islands of Aegina and Salamis. The Greek capital will spread out before you from the Aegean Sea to the surrounding mountains and will hold your attention for a long time, and I do not doubt that. But when you have admired this beauty (although it's hard to get enough of it), you will be able to see the Church of Saint George – a small and quite charming church built in the late 18th century on the site of an even older, possibly medieval church, about which we have only a symbolic idea. Opposite the church is a mechanized bell tower, striking the required number of strokes at strictly regulated times, and a flagpole flying the flag of the Greek Republic. At sunset and sunrise every day, three soldiers of the Greek army climb up to Lycabettus and perform the ceremony of raising (at sunrise) and lowering (at sunset) the national flag, as required by the

View of Athens from Lycabettus Hill.

regulations. A similar ceremony, however, is more elaborate and involves the singing of the anthem, carried out at the top of the Acropolis daily by soldiers of the Evzones regiment. A little further from the church and opposite the exit from the funicular station is the "Sky Bar," and I cannot recommend it to you. I think it has unreasonably high prices and has provided subpar service for the past five years. Still, if you climb up to Lycabettus at a less crowded time (such as a weekday morning), you can drink a coffee cup quite nicely, sitting at a table overlooking the awakening Athens.

One of the paths on Lycabettus Hill.

Practical Tips and Best (in my humble opinion)

Taverns, Cafés, and Bars.

Where is the best place to stay in Athens?
This question is crucial when planning your trip. Formulating an answer to it, I concluded that recommending specific hotels would be rash, as they tend to close down, and many of us prefer short-term apartment rentals. So, I decided to compile a list of the best neighborhoods for short-term stays, equally close to Athens' main attractions and transportation hubs.

- **Koukaki and Makryanni**: These two small neighborhoods are between Andrea Siggrou Avenue and the hills of Filopappou and Acropolis. They offer a vast selection of apartments for short-term rentals and hotels of various levels. The abundance of cafés, bars, and restaurants, proximity to the Acropolis and the old town, as well as being just ten minutes away from the Sigrou-Fix metro station (red line) and bus and trolley stops, make these neighborhoods among the best for your temporary stay. However, if you decide to stay here, it's best to start searching for accommodation in advance, as the best apartments and hotel rooms in these areas are quickly taken.

- **Filopappou:** This neighbourhood is located behind the hill of the same name, opposite the Athens Acropolis. It differs from its neighbors, Koukaki and Makryanni, only in its slightly greater distance from the old city center, but otherwise, it's quite decent.

- **Mets:** One of the ideal neighborhoods, in my opinion. Within walking distance, you'll find such wonderful attractions as the Panathenaic Stadium (Kallimarmaro), the Temple of Olympian Zeus (and right behind it, the old town), the First Athens Cemetery with its stunning open-air sculpture museum, and more. Several trolleybus and bus routes pass through this area, as well as a tram line connecting Mets to Syntagma Square and the coastal districts of Faliro and Glyfada, as well as the port of Piraeus (although I recommend getting to Piraeus by metro from Syntagma). If you choose to stay here, make sure to visit the jazz café "Mets" located on Markou

Mousourou Street, which occasionally hosts live music performances.

- **Pagrati (Pangrati):** The neighboring district of Athens is also exceptional in terms of cleanliness and has a variety of excellent taverns, cafés, and restaurants to suit every taste. Additionally, short-term rentals in this area should be slightly cheaper than in Mets, and due to Pagrati's size, there's more choice. This neighborhood is directly adjacent to the Panathenaic Stadium (Kallimarmaro) on one side and King George II Avenue, leading to the Royal Garden and the residence of the Greek Prime Minister on the other. Several trolleybuses and bus routes pass through it, but be careful: part of the road on their route is currently under construction, and the trolleybuses are being diverted.
- **Agios Nikolaos:** A neighborhood adjacent to Pagrati (considered by many Athenians as part of it). It's important not to confuse this Agios Nikolaos with another neighborhood in Athens on the Green metro line, which has turned into an immigrant ghetto in recent years, and which I strongly advise against. The Agios Nikolaos we need is located between King Constantine I Avenue and Imitou and Ulofa Palme streets. It houses one of the best hotels in Athens, the five-star "Divani Caravel." This neighbourhood is near the National Art Gallery and the Evangelismos metro station (blue line). Several trolleybus and bus routes also pass through it.
- **Kolonaki:** One of Athens's most expensive and prestigious (if not the most expensive and prestigious) neighbourhoods. It is located near the Parliament building (Old Royal Palace) and the Syntagma metro station, as well as at the foot of Mount Lycabettus, the highest point in the city. In this neighborhood, there are many decent and sometimes not very expensive establishments, but be careful: in the center of Kolonaki, on Filikis Eterias Square, construction of the fourth metro line is underway, so I wouldn't recommend staying near this square.
- **Monastiraki and Psiri** are not the cleanest compared to the previous districts of the old city, but they are quite convenient if you plan on walking a lot and visiting the main attractions. Moreover, these areas offer a huge selection of hotels, hostels, and hotels to suit every taste and daily rent. In addition, Psiri has many excellent cafes and

taverns (my recommendation is "Bougatsadiko Psirri" – a cafe with a pleasant atmosphere, where they prepare traditional Thessaloniki's "bougatsa" with minced meat and many other masterpieces of Greek cuisine from various types of dough. These areas are connected to other parts of the city by two metro stations ("Monastiraki" green line and "Monastiraki" blue line), but buses and trolleys hardly pass through them.

- **Plaka** – a large part of the old city is in this district. It is almost entirely pedestrianized and, therefore, quite quiet. By staying in Plaka, you will be able to see the main attractions of the city without resorting to public transport, but because the district is adjacent to Monastiraki on one side and the Acropolis on the other, all three branches of the Athens metro will be at your service. I can't recommend any taverns in Plaka, but the bar "Vrettos" ("Brettos") and the ice cream cafe "DaVinci Gelato" will not leave you indifferent.
- **Thissio** – a district located on the north side of Filopappou Hill, is also quite pleasant to live: many taverns, bars, cafes, the Thissio metro station on the Green line, and all the main attractions of the old city within walking distance. So, this would be my rating of districts for short stays in Athens. In many guidebooks and tourist websites, you can find information about cheap and decent hotels and apartments in the Omonia, Metaxourgio, Polytechnio, Victoria, and Exarchia districts. Still, I implore you: don't fall for it! Unfortunately, these areas are far from the most pleasant, clean, and safe parts of the city, and a small savings on daily rent or hotel room hire will not be worth ruining your vacation.

How to use public transport?

The most convenient and never-failing mode of transport for me has been and remains the Athens metro. It consists of three lines:

- **No. 1 (Green):** Piraeus-Kifisia. It connects the port city of Piraeus with the northern suburb of Kifisia and passes through almost the entire old center (Thissio, Monastiraki, Omonia, Victoria). Along this line, you can easily reach the National Archaeological Museum of Athens (closest to Victoria station), but beware: it is inhabited by many unpleasant characters, and cases of pickpocketing are not uncommon.

- **No. 2 (Red):** Anthoupoli-Elliniko. It connects two Athenian suburbs (northwest and southeast) and passes through both the old center (Metaxourgio, Omonia) and Syntagma Square and the Acropolis (Acropolis station).
- **No. 3 (Blue):** Dimotiko Theatro – Doukissis Plakentias – Airport. It is the most interesting and longest line of the Athens metro. The main part connects the northern suburb of Athens (Doukissis Plakentias station) with the port city of Piraeus (Piraeus and Dimotiko Theatro stations). However, every 34-35 minutes from Piraeus, trains depart to Athens International Airport "Eleftherios Venizelos," you can easily get there for 9 euros, saving on a taxi.

Metro tickets can be purchased both at the ticket office and at special machines, where you can also choose any of your preferred languages (English, French, German, Italian, Arabic, Greek, or Russian). Suppose you intend to travel around Athens beyond the mentioned pedestrian routes. In that case, you can buy so-called "tourist tickets" with unlimited trips on all types of public transport (bus, trolleybus, tram, metro), valid for 72 hours from purchase and including one trip to the airport. Such a ticket will cost you 20 euros. If you need to use the metro or other public

transport no more than once, your choice is a single ticket valid for 90 minutes, during which you can make unlimited transfers. It will cost you 1.20 euros. You can also buy a ticket with unlimited rides on all types of transport, valid for 5 days, but it will not include trips on the metro to the airport or on bus X90, which goes to the airport from Syntagma Square. Such a ticket costs 8.20 euros. Important! You cannot buy tickets from a bus, trolley bus, or tram driver, and ticket vending machines or active ticket offices are not available at every stop, so it's better to deal with tickets immediately at one of the metro stations.

Where and what to eat best?

This question worries us almost as much as the previous ones, doesn't it? Well, you've come to the right place: I love eating almost as much as history, so I'm happy to present my list of the most delicious and affordable establishments, many of which unfairly lack attention from other guidebooks and tourist websites.

Taverns and restaurants:

- **Alexandrino Kebab Pagrati** – a completely charming tavern in every respect, with the most delicious Greek kebab in Constantinople style (Politiko Kebab), grilled halloumi cheese, and, of course, Cretan salad "Dakos." The area of Pagrati, as well as the areas lying north of it – Vironas, Kesariani, and Kareas, in the 1920s, were settled by Greek and Armenian refugees from Turkey, fleeing the genocide of the Christian population of the former Ottoman Empire by Mustafa Kemal's army. They brought their music, their dialect of the Greek language, and, of course, their cuisine. And "Politiko Kebab" (which translates to "City Kebab" because the Greeks of Constantinople colloquially called their native city simply "Polis" – "City") is one of the brightest representatives of this culinary tradition. If you suddenly think that kebab is a Turkish dish, dismiss these thoughts because kebabs were prepared in Ancient Greece even in the time of Homer and even earlier, as evidenced by numerous archaeological finds of special grills and kebab sticks. This dish was called "obelos" in ancient Greek, but over time, this word was replaced by the Arabic-Turkish "kebab". **Establishment address: Imitou 90 &, Ifikratous, Athina 116 34**
- **To Gnision** – another excellent Anatolian (Eastern Greek) cuisine establishment opened its doors in 1922. I can say the same about "Alexandrino Kebab Pagrati": you will not be disappointed if you choose this place to explore the full range of tastes and aromas of Greek culinary traditions. **Establishment address: Imittou 50, Kesariani 161 21**
- **Mavro Provato of Press Café** – a place where you can try unexpected dishes of Greek cuisine not served in traditional taverns, such as Kleftiko – a specially prepared lamb with potatoes. Like the previous two, tourists do not often visit this establishment; nevertheless, they provide an English menu. But be careful: if you want to go to this place on Friday, Saturday, or Sunday (and any other day of the week, perhaps), it's better to reserve a table in advance, as it is consistently popular among Athenians. **Establishment address: Arrianou 33, Athina 116 35**
- **Mailo's** – in case you get tired of Greek cuisine (which I don't believe in any way) or get hungry, and there's not a single decent tavern

nearby. I confidently recommend this network of small restaurants serving the best pasta in Athens. **Establishment addresses: Eratosthenous 30, Athina 116 35 | Patriarchou Ioakim 39, Athina 106 75 | Falirou 3, Athina 117 42 | Athinaidos 11, Athina 105 63**

- **Karamanlidika** – if what I eat at this establishment for lunch turns out to be my last meal, then I will be the fullest and happiest ghost in the world. Karamanlides were the sub-ethnic group of Greeks who lived on the Anatolian Peninsula from time immemorial (like the Pontic Greeks), but unlike their fellow countrymen who settled in the interior of the continent rather than along the coast, which predetermined their "Turkization": by the beginning of the 20th century, the vast majority of Karamanlides, although Orthodox and using the Greek script, still spoke Turkish. The center of Karamanlid culture was the city of Karaman, which in ancient times was called Larinda in Greek. After the defeat of the Greek Kingdom in the Second Greco-Turkish War of 1919-1922 and the population exchange between Turkey and Greece, a result of which 1.5 million Orthodox subjects of the former Ottoman Empire were resettled here, and 500,000 Muslims were evicted from Greece, almost all Karamanlides found themselves on their historical homeland. Over the past century, the descendants of this small sub-ethnic group have been completely assimilated with the local Greeks. Still, in this unique establishment, you can experience their culture through their cuisine called "Karamanlidika." Mandatory for tasting: "Itsli Kefte" – meatballs made of semolina with minced meat filling; Karamanlid-style chickpeas with basturma; bulgur with mushrooms, oranges, turmeric, and graviera cheese; Karamanlid sausage "parmak" and much more. **Establishment address: Evripidou 52, Athina 105 52**

- **Avli** – a very charming classic tavern located in the enclosed inner courtyard of an old house, which makes it difficult to find, but believe me, it's worth it. No matter how many times I've been there, I can say that the atmosphere there is the most Athenian. **Establishment address: Ag. Dimitriou 12, Athina 105 54 (a small door under an inconspicuous green sign).**

- **The Greco's Project** – I don't like it when they try to make haute cuisine out of Greek cuisine, but I can't help but recommend you to have a cup of traditional Greek espresso – "Ellinikos kafes," prepared in hot ash and served with a shot of rose liqueur in traditional dishes. This preparation method is called "se hovoli" – "in ash," it's an exceptional pleasure. **Establishment address: Evaggelistrias 9, Athina 105 63**

- **Veganaki** – the perfect choice if you are vegan and want to try something traditional. Greek Sudzukakia – traditional chickpea meatballs baked in the oven in a sauce of tomatoes, cumin, and garlic, will not leave you indifferent. **Establishment address: Athanasiou Diakou 38, Athina 117 43**

Cafés:

- **Metz** – located in the eponymous district, known as "Athens's Montmartre": the first jazz cafes in the Greek capital appeared in the Metz area, where many Greek actors, directors, poets, writers, artists, and musicians of the 1950s gathered. Although this café did not witness those times, it still strives to preserve the traditions of its place: sometimes, small Greek jazz bands perform there. Be sure to try the hot chocolate with strawberries if you visit. **Address: Mark. Mousourou 63, Athens 116 36**
- **Melina Mercouri Café** – opened in memory of one of the great Greek actresses, the first woman Minister of Culture of Greece, and the companion of the life of the French director Jules Dassin, her good friend, this café will transport you to the romantic and magical world of 1950s cinema, and they also serve the tastiest pancakes with various fillings and traditional Greek mountain herb tea. **Address: Lisiou 22, Athens 105 56**
- **Bougatsadiko Psirri** is a wonderful cafe bakery that has been baking Thessaloniki "bugatsa" with meat filling and has been brewing delicious coffee for many years. Additionally, you can try salepi – a traditional Eastern warming drink made from orchid root, honey, cinnamon, and ginger. Of course, salepi is best enjoyed in winter: nothing warms you up on a damp Athenian December like it. **Address: Pl. Iroon 1, Athens 105 54**
- **Veneti Great Baggeion** – another café-bakery that opened in the restored part of the once fashionable Bagion hotel on Omonia Square – one of Ernst Ziller's architectural masterpieces. In this establishment, carefully recreated the frescoes made during the building's construction in the second half of the 19th century, a beautiful

mezzanine with tables above the main hall creates a tranquil atmosphere of a 1950s Parisian café, and the delicious desserts, pastries, and coffee will set your mood for the whole day. **Address: Pl. Omonias 18, Athens 105 52**

- **Veneti Bakery 1948 NEON** – located on the same Omonia Square as "Veneti Great Bageion" and belonging to the same network of Athenian café-bakeries, but "Neon" itself is one of the most famous, at one time, cafés in the city, where the cream of the interwar (1922-1940) and post-war (after 1945) Athenian society gathered. One of the most famous Greek artists, Yiannis Tsarouchis, depicted "Neon" in two of his paintings, exhibited in the National Gallery of Athens. In 2010, the old café went bankrupt, after which the "Veneti" chain bought it out, and, after careful restoration and revival of the atmosphere of old Athens, it reopened its doors to visitors. Vintage photographs on the walls, chess tables, neoclassical interiors, and exact replicas of tables and chairs from the early 20th century, which stood here before the first closure: all this is simply magical. **Address: Pl. Omonias 7, Athina 104 31**

- **Loumidis** – perhaps not a classic café, but they prepare exceptional coffee there. The first shop of the current "Loumidis" chain opened in 1920. In a few years, it managed to gain immense popularity among Athenians, offering the best roasted and ground coffee by weight. The most famous blend of this brand is "Papagalos" – "Parrot," and this bird has also become the company's emblem. The history of such a strange symbol for a coffee shop is simple: the very first shop of the Lumidis brothers opened on the premises of a former studio, and "inheritance" from the previous owners of the café was clean advertising leaflets with the logo of this very studio – a colorful parrot. In this same shop, you can buy an unusual souvenir as a memory of Athens – local branded coffee beans or a small coffee set with the company's logo, "Loumidis." **Address: Aiolou 106, Athens 105 64**

Bars:
- **Old fashioned bar** – one of Athens's most atmospheric drinking establishments – opened its doors to visitors in 2004. Its owner knows a thing or two about jazz, blues, and rock, and an evening spent in

this place will surely leave you with vivid memories of the Greek capital. **Address: Miaouli 16, Athina 105 54**

- **Beertime** – here, you can try almost all types of Greek beer (yes, Greece has many large and small breweries). Rhodes, Crete, Peloponnese, Athens, Thessaloniki, Naxos – lessons in Greek geography have never been more fascinating! **Address: Pl. Iroon 1, Athina 105 54**

- **James Joyce Pub** – the best Irish pub in Athens and a gathering place for the English, Irish, and Scottish communities. Every Champions League game is a major event in the life of the neighborhood where this bar is located. **Address: Astiggos 12, Athina 105 55**

- **Berlin by 5 drunk men** – a bar where you can pour your beer from taps on your tables. It has been a gathering place for residents of the Pagrati district and adjacent parts of Athens for decades. It is an excellent place for those who want to meet the "locals" and feel the city from the inside out. **Address: Timotheou 8, Athina 116 33**

IMPORTANT!

Holidays and other days when shops, some cafes, and bars may be closed, and the city center may be blocked off:

- **May 1st** – Labour Day (demonstrations and strikes may occur, disrupting public transport).
- **May 3rd** – Good Friday (a holiday of the Greek Orthodox Church).
- **May 4th** – Holy Saturday (a holiday of the Greek Orthodox Church).
- **May 5th** – Easter (a holiday of the Greek Orthodox Church).
- **June 24th** – Feast of the Holy Spirit.
- **August 15th** – Assumption of the Virgin Mary.
- **October 28th** – "No" (Ohi) Day (start of the Greco-Italian War).
- **November 17th** – Polytechnic Uprising Day in Athens (this day sees demonstrations by left-wing radical activists in central areas near the University, often escalating into mass riots, so be cautious on this day).
- **December 6th** – On this day, left-wing radical activists also hold mass demonstrations in central areas of the city (Omonia, Exarchia, Victoria, Akadimias, Syntagma).
- **December 25th** – Christmas.
- **December 26th** – Synaxis of the Most Holy Theotokos.

Afterword.

Athens is an ancient, tired, sleepy city plagued by crises, wars, and natural disasters, but despite everything, it retains some magical charm. You will feel it somewhere in the narrow, winding streets of Plaka, or feel its gentle touch along with the wind at the top of Lycabettus, or hear it amidst the hustle and bustle of the market streets, but you will find it. This city closes itself off to those who come to it thoughtlessly, but before those willing to listen to the quiet voice of its dusty ruins, it opens up in all its ancient grace. And I want to believe that my guide helped you get to know Athens in a way that, when you return home, you will answer your friends' questions about the trip with: "It's a city with a soul." After all, it truly has one, and it is given to you, travelers, much more than any of the locals, to see it and live through all 4000 years of Athens' history with them in just a few days. Isn't that real magic?

See you on the next journey.
Yours sincerely,
G. Esperidis.

Made in the USA
Las Vegas, NV
07 November 2024

11311755R00105